THE PROG RAMMER

MICHAEL DI LORETO

authorHOUSE®

AuthorHouse™
1663 Liberty Drive
Bloomington, IN 47403
www.authorhouse.com
Phone: 833-262-8899

Published by AuthorHouse   01/03/2025

ISBN: 979-8-8230-4028-0 (sc)
ISBN: 979-8-8230-4027-3 (e)

Library of Congress Control Number: 2024927138

Print information available on the last page.

CONTENTS

PREFACE

In the early days of computers, people became Programmers in many different ways. They didn't get Computer Science degrees and then get hired as Software Engineers like people do now. They mostly had degrees in other subjects and had jobs doing something else when their companies bought their first computer and they happened to get to work on them. Each person seemed to have their own different story about how they became a Programmer by chance. My own story is like that, except that I didn't go to college and I didn't have another career.

Young people now plan their careers in advance. I never did. In high school I had no idea what I wanted to do. I never even considered going to college. I didn't know anyone who went to college, and I always just thought that was for other maybe wealthy people. My family was poor, but we didn't notice it because we had what we needed. I think my mother struggled with money, but she didn't let her three kids know about it. Teenagers, and even younger children, are always asked what they want to be when they grow up. I didn't know. I didn't want to be anything. Of course, nobody ever asked me if I wanted to be a Computer Programmer.

It was just a random sequence of events that landed me in a programming class, and then a little later into my first programming job. I wasn't ambitious, I had no plan, things just happened. Once I was in my first job, I was so interested in it that I worked hard and learned and became very good at it. That led to other jobs, and so on.

This is the story of my programming career. It's mostly about my jobs, computers and programming. There's not much personal in it because my personal life is mostly stupid and embarrassing, and really not interesting. Besides talking about my work experiences, which were actually very good, I give what I think of as lessons for Programmers. They are not technical lessons, but more like observations about what programming is like, and conclusions about how to do programming well. It's self-centered, of course, from my own unique point of view. I address myself directly to other Programmers or to people who want to be Programmers.

Michael Di Loreto
Programmer
Las Vegas
2024

CHAPTER 1

1968

A Strange Way To Become
A Programmer

I WAS DEPORTED from Palm Springs. Well, maybe not deported. Banished maybe, or exiled? Whatever. I was sent from Palm Springs where I lived with my mother to Los Angeles to live with my father. It was 1968. I was 17 years old.

My father, Robert Di Loreto, was a Computer Programmer. He was currently working for a company that had a UNIVAC 9300 computer. He had been doing that at least since I was a child, working for UNIVAC itself when it was called Remington Rand. He worked on the UNIVAC Solid State 90 computer. So he had connections. He arranged for me to take a one-week class there in RPG programming that June. I don't know how he did it, but he knew the teacher.

At that time computers were so expensive that UNIVAC included the software, manuals, training and support for free. The classes didn't cost anything, but they were not open to the public. They were for customers and their own employees. I was the only one in the class who was neither one, and I was the only one who was not already in the business and knew absolutely nothing about computers. On the first day, I had to ask what a "card" was.

The UNIVAC Data Center was on Wilshire Blvd. in the Wilshire District. The company my father worked for, Daniel Mann Johnson & Mendenhall, DMJM, pronounced DimJim, was also there a couple of blocks away. My father's apartment was in easy walking distance.

I took to programming right away. When my first program was ready, my father took me to his office and let me run it on their UNIVAC 9300 computer. In those days, a program was punched into 80-column cards. The computer was not very large for that time. There was a central processor with a printer on the left and a card reader on the right in a kind of an L shape. The whole ensemble was about chest high. The console was a large panel of lights and switches. You stood to operate it. To run a program, you put your deck of cards in the card reader, flipped a switch on the console, pushed a button, flipped the switch back again and pushed another button. The computer made a powerful humming sound, the card reader made a loud racket, then it was still for several seconds with just the lights blinking. Finally, the printer started to print. It was really exciting to see my first program running and the results printing.

Does that sound lame? You're reading this because you're also a Programmer or you're interested in programming. So, you probably have a laptop on your desk that makes very little noise and has no blinking lights, just a keyboard, a mouse and a monitor. You don't get the experience of running a big, loud machine in its own special computer room. Too bad.

UNIVAC® 9300 System with Uniservo VI C Tape Units

At the end of the week, the teacher invited the class to come back for a 3-week Assembler Language class. I volunteered, and they let me. My father also joined the class. These two classes were about the UNIVAC 9200/9300 computers, so it was the same as the computer at my father's job. I never had the feeling he was supervising me, but I think he took the class because I did. I didn't sit with him. I sat next to a guy named Ron Buffington who was a UNIVAC employee. In those three weeks, Ron and I talked a little bit, although not much because I was very shy, and we even worked on a class problem together.

At the end of the two classes I was a Computer Programmer. I even tried to get a job as a Programmer. I went to a couple of interviews, but they were companies with IBM computers, and I had no experience or qualifications at all. Obviously, I didn't get hired.

When I turned 18 in September of that year, I was allowed to go back to Palm Springs. I got a job washing cars at a used car lot. I was only there about a week when my mother showed up at the car lot to tell me I had a programming job in L.A. I immediately went in to the manager and told him I quit. He didn't like that and told me he would not give me a reference. Fine.

CHAPTER 2

1968 - 1969

Guidance Technology, Inc

S O, I TOOK a bus back to L.A. and stayed in my father's apartment again. The job was in Santa Monica at a company called Guidance Technology, Inc. (GTI). I never knew what the company did. I never even went into the very large factory-like building. I only ever went into their computer center where they had a new UNIVAC 9300 computer. To manage the computer center, they hired UNIVAC employee Ron Buffington, the same guy I say next to in the Assembler Language class, and he hired me. I was a full-time trainee Programmer just turned 18.

As usual, I didn't know how that happened. I didn't ask and nobody told me. I just assumed my father had some influence and convinced Ron to give me a chance. I don't believe my father had any kind of power over him. It's just that the world around UNIVAC computers was pretty small and everyone knew everyone else and they tended to help each other. Still, why would a new manager hire someone's kid just because they asked you to?

Here's how I got the title of my story, *The Programmer*. I borrowed it from *The Godfather*. In the movie, the Godfather is an older man well established in his position with a lot of respect and influence. But the story is really about his son who becomes the new Godfather and takes it to a much higher level. Our fathers were both Italian and we were both named Michael. Other than that, we really have nothing in common at all.

My father was a Programmer for a long time in the world around UNIVAC computers and had a very good reputation. He arranged for me to take my first programming class and later he arranged for me to get my first programming job, which turned into a 49-year career in some of the most advanced technology companies including, yes, UNIVAC, but also Data General, the NASA Jet Propulsion Laboratory (JPL), Silicon Graphics Inc. (SGI), Hewlett-Packard (HP), Oracle Corporation and many more.

Naturally, I think I should get some of the credit. In class, I was serious, attentive, polite, intelligent and good-looking. Ron Buffington saw me sitting next to him every day for three weeks. He didn't just blindly hire some colleague's kid. He knew me. He knew what I was like.

I worked hard. I learned like a sponge. At GTI, we used both RPG and the Assembler Language. The senior Programmer was Fred Bartlett, who had been a co-worker of my father at DMJM. I learned some technical things from him for sure, but the only thing I really remember him saying was: *"More Thought, Less Code."* I followed that principle the rest of my career.

In about three months, I was promoted to Programmer and I got a raise to $3.00/hr. When I started, I got $2.64/hr. That doesn't sound like much, but compared to my job at the used car lot where I got the minimum wage of $1.65/hr., I thought I was rich. Some time later I think I got up to $3.25/hr. That's about $500/mo., pretty good for an 18-year-old in 1969.

I also served as a computer operator. In the beginning, the Programmers ran their own programs. I did too, but I also ran jobs for other people. Within a few months, they hired a full-time computer operator. Even then, I still ran some production jobs for customers. We had a customer who had their own small computer data processing business, but they didn't have their own computer. The two owners came to our office and used our computer. One time, I did a contract programming job for them. I sat with the president of the company to find out what he wanted the new program to do. He explained it to me, gave me information about the input, and I designed the report on a form we had for printer layouts. It was a typical RPG program that read cards for input and printed a report. As usual for a business report, it had detail lines, sub-totals, totals and a grand total. The man told me he wanted the grand total to print on top of the first page. I said I could do that, but normally the totals are accumulated as the report is printing, and the grand total is at the end. You would have to process all the data twice to print the grand total first. He understood, and let me do it my way. This trivial anecdote is to me actually very important for computer software development in general. *You can negotiate requirements.*

Together with my story about computers I knew and things I did, I also want to include the most important lessons I learned along the way. This is one of them. There is a huge amount of information about software development printed in books and presented at conferences. The software development process is usually broken down into analysis, design and programming. The analysis part, done by a software professional who is not necessarily a Programmer, is where the analyst gathers requirements from the customer and generally lays out what a program is going to do. This will often be the basis for a contract with the customer. The analyst produces a reasonable estimate of the size of the project, the cost, the amount of time, and so on, and the customer agrees to go ahead. Then, the program is designed by a Programmer. Where the analysis and contract say what do to, the design says how to do it. This would include the identification of tools and other resources to accomplish the goal. The design would be documented and approved by the customer. Finally, the program would be written. When that's done and working, there would be a demonstration for the customer to show that all the agreed-on requirements are satisfied, which leads to the most important part, getting paid.

If you've ever read a book about software development methodology, it probably says something like that. Unfortunately, these days the analysis and design parts seem to be mostly gone, especially if you're practicing Agile programming. Then it's all just coding.

The point I want to make, though, is that the requirements part of the process sometimes doesn't work. Someone gathering requirements might ask the customer what they want, the customer tells them, and they write it down. Then, it seems to be set in stone. The requirements are the requirements. They are *required*. You have to do what they say. I've seen major projects fail that way. Not any projects I was in charge of, by the way. I knew better right from my very first project on my very first job. I've also seen Programmers complain that the customers don't know what they want, and that's why the project was in trouble. I see it the other way around. It's the Analyst's job to help the customer to determine what they want. The customer might not be a technology expert. They might not know what's feasible or even possible. Asking someone what they want, and then just taking it as *required* does not lead to the best results.

The computer room at GTI was really great. It had a raised floor, air conditioning, and windows on two sides with our cubicles on the outside. There was the UNIVAC 9300 computer with its card reader and printer. It also had a card punch and five magnetic tape drives. Four of them were 9-track tapes and one was 7-track. The 7-track tape was used to transfer printed reports to a big offline print station. In the room were also a card sorter, a card collator and a big machine for decollating multiple-copy printed reports. There were also three or four keypunch machines. Later, a big machine for reading paper tape was installed.

One of my part-time operator jobs was to produce some huge report. It involved running a program on the 9300 computer that wrote the report onto a 7-track tape. Then I took the tape to the offline print station to print it. The report was on two copies with carbon paper in between. Then I took the printed report to the decollating machine to separate the copies and dispose of the carbon paper. The offline print station was very fast and often jammed. The decollating machine was even faster and jammed even more. It was a very difficult job because I would start it printing and it would jam. I would fix the jam and start it again, and it would jam again. Eventually, when that was done, I put the printed report in the decollating machine which would jam even faster. It was difficult to fix the jams in both machines because of the multiple parts and the carbon paper. It was not just one printed report. While I was decollating one report, I was printing another one. And while I was doing that, I was running the computer to make another tape for the printer. At first, I could only do one of the three steps at a time. Eventually, I got to where I could have all three machines running at once. Do you believe in psychic power over machines? I think I had it.

I really liked having hands on the machines. I had a close connection to them. Even though an Operator was generally considered to be a lower level job than a Programmer, I always wanted to run the machines myself. Another thing I liked to do was to write programs to try things. I made up technical challenges for myself, and then wrote programs just to learn things. I called them *play programs*. My interest in learning how computers work at the most fundamental levels possible led me to write my own single-card program for the UNIVAC 9300. It was modelled after the card bootstrap loader that came with the machine. The way the bootstrap loader worked was that you flipped a switch on the computer front panel and pushed a button. The computer would read one card that contained binary instruction code into memory. You flipped the switch the other way, and pressed the *run* button, and the computer would start executing the code from that card. That code in turn would read a whole program on cards into memory, and then run the program. So, I wrote my own one-card program that didn't do any more than just get control, display something on the front panel lights and stop. That's all. But to do that, I had to write the binary machine code myself and then keypunch that into a card. The keypunch machine had a multi-punch feature that allowed me to key in binary code. My small program worked on the bare machine.

Does that make sense? Was I supposed to do that? Did anybody tell me I could do that? Well, no. It's just that I was a Programmer because I loved computers and programming. From then on, all through my career, I always wrote *play programs*. I always wanted to know how things worked and how to do things. Even though it wasn't ever on any job description, I thought my job was to learn. That made me the expert who knew computers and software inside out and who could solve most any problem. What was fun to me actually turned out to be very significant in solving real problems and finishing real projects. By doing things my employers didn't necessarily want me to do, I became all that much more valuable to them.

MICHAEL DI LORETO

The UNIVAC 9300 was a 16-bit machine, that is, it had 16-bit registers, but it could also access memory in 8-bit bytes. The instruction set was about the same as the IBM 360/20, and the character code was the same as IBM's EBCDIC.

The UNIVAC 9300 was a third generation computer, and so was the IBM 360. The computer generations didn't mean much to Programmers. It had something to do with the types of electronics because there were major differences. The first generation computers used vacuum tubes. If you're old enough you'll remember the tubes in television sets. Examples of first generation computers were the UNIVAC I and UNIVAC II. The second generation used transistors. Examples of second generation computers were the UNIVAC 418 and 490 series of computers and the UNIVAC 1050. The third generation had integrated circuits.

Since my father was a Programmer before me, I think I can call myself a Second Generation Programmer. In the early days of my career, I might have been the only one, or at least one of a very few. I was born in 1950, the same year as the UNIVAC I, so my history shares a lot with computer history. As a child in the 1950s, my father took me to his office where I was allowed to play with the card sorting machine. Seems like I was born to be a Programmer.

When GTI got a paper tape reading machine, I was assigned to make it work. All I had to do was to write a program to read the paper tape and write the data on a magnetic tape for input to other programs later. It sounds simple, but the machine was new and very temperamental. It was so fast that the first time my program tried to read the paper tape it shot the tape clear across the room. It took a lot of trial and error to get it to work right at all. This task was the first time I did programming that was not for a business application. It was a kind of special-purpose utility program. That's important to me because I would do a lot of this kind of thing later. Whenever there was a need for some unusual kind of program, I would be the one to do it. I never knew whether the companies picked me to do these things because no one else wanted to do them. I like to believe it was because I was the best at it and most likely to get it done.

I think I was really lucky to learn so many valuable lessons on my very first job. The concept of RPG programming would mean a lot to me later. Assembler Language programming gave me deep insight into the fundamental way computers work, which was also very useful later. Negotiating requirements, play programming, and special-purpose utility programming would all be very important to my projects throughout my career.

I was at GTI about a year when they shut down the computer center. What happened was that computers were so expensive the company thought they could lower their cost by selling computer time. I think this idea probably came from the UNIVAC salesman because I know of other companies that did the same thing. I never heard the reason, but I guess the cost was too high and the income from selling computer time wasn't what they expected.

CHAPTER 3

1969 - 1970

Computer Communications Network

R ON BUFFINGTON WENT to work at another UNIVAC installation, California Computer Communications Network (CCN) in Torrance. This was a new branch of the Nashville, Tennessee company, Computer Communications Network. He didn't hire me, but I think he must have recommended me because I got a job there too. Of course, other UNIVAC people who worked there also knew my father which made me more acceptable. Naturally, I think it was more to do with my record of good work at GTI and my intelligent appearance, but who knows?

CCN had two large UNIVAC 418-II Real-Time Systems that they wanted to use to provide online business services to other companies. The 418-II was a second generation computer. It had 64k 18-bit words of core memory. I learned the Assembler Language, which was called ART (Assembler for Real-Time), but I didn't do any real work with it.

CCN had the whole top floor of a Wells Fargo Bank building in the Torrance Financial Center. The computer room was really like three computer rooms that were open to each other. Two of the rooms each had a UNIVAC 418-II system and the third one had an IBM 360/30 and some other equipment. Each 418-II had two gigantic FASTRAND drums. Each one weighed over 2 tons and was I think about 6 feet high and 8 feet long. Each 418-II also had an FH-880 Flying Head Drum, which was also very large. There were also rows of magnetic tape drives, card readers, printers, and so on. The 418-II had a teletype console.

UNIVAC specialized in Real-Time Systems. In those days, Real Time meant human time. When you did a transaction in a bank, for example, the teller could use a terminal connected to a UNIVAC computer to make a deposit or check your balance immediately while you stood there. That was Real Time. That was in contrast to batch processing, which was what most computers were used for. Transactions were accumulated during the day, and then processed overnight. The motto UNIVAC used at that time was "NOW". Of course, these days interacting with a computer in human time is normal, and "real-time" means something entirely different.

4. COMPONENT DESCRIPTION

4.1. GENERAL PROCESSOR

Figure 4–1. Central Processor

CHARACTERISTICS	
STORAGE CAPACITY	4,096 words to 65,536 words
WORD LENGTH	18 bits plus parity bit
NUMBER OF I/O CHANNELS	8, 12 or 16
CYCLE TIME	2 Microseconds
AVERAGE INSTRUCTION EXECUTION TIME	4 Microseconds

The UNIVAC 418-II Real-Time System has a core storage capacity of 65,536 words of 2 microsecond cycle time. This model is available in 4,096-word increments and can be field modified upward to its maximum capacity.

The UNIVAC 418-II Real-Time System Processor is designed for real time and batch processing; for satellite operations; for concurrency of operations; for the employment of advanced programming concepts such as those incorporated in the ART assembler, the executive routine, the various input/output routines; and for the use of extremely extensive and rapid mass random access storage and communications subsystems as well as magnetic tape auxiliary storage, punched card equipment, and a variety of special peripheral devices.

I worked on the Burroughs TC-500, which was advertised as the world's first intelligent terminal. It had its own language they called the GP-300 Communications Macro Assembler. My TC-500 programs were assembled on the 418-II and the object code was punched onto paper tape. The TC-500 loaded programs from paper tape. The TC-500 was like a small desk you could sit at with a keyboard, a printer, a paper tape reader and a network connection. It would be in a customer's office connected by a leased telephone line to the mainframe computer at the CCN office. The TC-500 had 64-bit words that were divided into 4 16-bit syllables. That's right, syllables. I don't know any other computer that used that term. Instructions were 16 bits. They were very powerful instructions that could do very high-level things like send a message or print a line on the printer. I think there were 512 words of program storage, but it's been awhile.

Working on an intelligent terminal computer was my first experience in computer communications. I learned how modems worked, but it was mostly pretty high level. Still, being involved in the communications between computers is something I would do a lot more of later, and I think that experience was very helpful. The concept of a very high level Assembler Language was also something I would use a lot in future projects.

Experience is a funny thing. Employers seek to hire someone who has experience relevant to the job they're hiring for. I didn't get a job at a place that wanted experience on an IBM 360/40 with DOS and their particular language and application. That was normal. For me, though, I used all my experience on computers with operating systems and languages that most people had never heard of, but was totally relevant to me. I just mentioned that my experience with the Burroughs TC-500 would be very helpful to me later on systems that were completely different. Maybe you don't believe me. It's difficult to explain how that worked.

I was only there for about 9 months when this company also failed and went out of business. I needed another job. Fortunately, Ron Buffington, got a job as the manager of the computer center at Western Gear Corp. in Lynwood, and he hired me again.

Burroughs TC 500

A new concept in terminals . . . a new approach to on-line systems design.

MICHAEL DI LORETO

CHAPTER 4

1970 - 1971

Western Gear Corporation

WESTERN GEAR HAD a UNIVAC 9400 computer. The 9400 is in the same line as the 9300 but much bigger. Where the 9300 was a 16-bit computer, the 9400 used 32-bit words. Instead of the maximum 32k bytes of memory on the 9300, the 9400 came with 131k. The 9400 had a big maintenance panel with lots of switches and colorful blinking lights, but the operations console was a keyboard and printer, like a typewriter but more modern looking. It also had big disk drives and a disk-based operating system they called OS/4.

The UNIVAC 9000 series computers were basically copied from the IBM 360 family of computers. By that I mean the instruction set architecture was basically the same. The electronics were all different. The OS/4 operating system was also a lot like IBM DOS except that it was a true multiprogramming operating system where DOS was single programming.

There were some interesting differences between the UNIVAC and IBM cultures. For instance, you might have noticed just now that I said the UNIVAC 9400 had 131k bytes of memory. For IBM, that would be 128k. Computer memory sizes were measured in kilobytes, which means thousands of bytes, but were really multiples of 1024 since that's a power of 2. So, where for IBM 128k means 128 x 1024 bytes, UNIVAC cleverly makes it 131k or 131 x 1000. They both come out to exactly 131,072 bytes, even though the UNIVAC one sounds bigger.

You might also notice I always use the word 'memory'. IBM computers used core memory and IBM people would refer to it as 'core' for short. UNIVAC 9000 series computers used plated-wire memory, not core. So, for example, an IBM person would say "core dump" where a UNIVAC person would say "memory dump". In about 1972, semiconductor memory instantly made every other memory technology obsolete. Still, even many years later, people would use the word 'core' to refer to the computer memory even on computers not made by IBM.

On last thing I'll mention about the different cultures. When I asked what a "card" was, I was referring to a punched card also known as an 80-column card. Many people called those things "IBM cards". UNIVAC didn't like that. I think UNIVAC actually invented the punched card, originally with 90 columns. Maybe IBM was the one that changed it to 80 columns and deserved to have them called "IBM cards", but no UNIVAC person would ever say that.

I was the Systems Programmer at Western Gear. I don't know if a job title like that exists anymore, so I'll explain what I think it meant. In those days, the operating system was written in the Assembler Language for the particular computer and was delivered in source code. That code then had to be configured for the individual installation with the selection of optional software components, things like the number and type of disk and tape drives, and all kinds of parameters. That process was called System Generation, or SYSGEN. The Systems Programmer was the onsite expert who configured, built and maintained the operating system.

I was also a COBOL programmer. Their applications had already been developed for a UNIVAC 1108 computer and the job then for me and the other Programmers was to convert the programs from UNIVAC 1108 COBOL to UNIVAC 9400 COBOL. It was real work. They're not the same. My part was the Accounts Payable System.

MICHAEL DI LORETO

Figure 1—1. The UNIVAC 9400 System

1.3. SYSTEM CONFIGURATION

The processor (see Figure 1—2) includes main storage, control, arithmetic, and input/output sections.

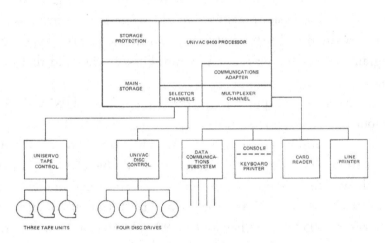

Figure 1—2. Block Diagram of a Typical System Configuration

    At GTI, I used RPG and the Assembler Language to develop business applications. These types of application programs mostly update files and print reports. RPG is especially well-suited to that kind of application, but not for general purpose programming. COBOL is also used for business applications, but it is much more general than RPG. We used Assembler Language for business applications on small computers with only 32k bytes of memory because a big programming language like COBOL was just not available.

Besides business applications there's another kind of programming I like to call utility programming. These are special purpose programs that are not directly for any business application, and they are usually more technical, requiring more expertise. A simple example might be to convert the format of a file to another format for a different computer.

As the Systems Programmer, I would also do utility programming, and to me it was part of the same role. The computer room had a raised floor and windows for people to see the computers inside. It was generally locked and not accessible to the programming staff. I was the only one who actually worked in the computer room, sitting at the computer console. I also had a cubicle like the other Programmers where I did my routine work. But for more technical things I was in the computer room. Besides maintaining the operating system, disks had to be formatted and space had to be manually allocated. Applications programs had to be put into a program library, and I did that for all the applications.

In the same computer room there was an old UNIVAC 1005 computer. That thing was a real antique. The UNIVAC 1004 computer was programmed by plugging wires into a big panel. To turn the 1004 into a 1005, the wiring panel was replaced by a big electronic module that allowed the computer to execute a program stored in memory. In their transition to the 9400, there were still files that could only be read by the 1005 because they were on 90-column cards. I wrote utility programs in the UNIVAC 1005 Assembler Language to transfer data to magnetic tape so that it could be read on the 9400. I also had to be in the computer room to operate the 1005.

The UNIVAC 1005 had 4 memory banks of 31 rows by 31 columns of 6-bit bytes. The character code was XS-3. I really enjoyed learning about different computers and programming them. And I was really fortunate to get to work on so many different things. Here I was in less than 3 years already with deep expertise on 4 different computers, UNIVAC 9300, 9400, 1005 and Burroughs TC-500, with Assembler Languages for all 4 plus RPG and COBOL.

Figure 2-2. UNIVAC 1005 System Model III

UNIVAC 1005 MODEL III

BASIC SYSTEM	SPEEDS
PROCESSOR	6.5 MICROSECOND CORE CYCLE TIME
READER	615 CARDS PER MINUTE
PRINTER	600 LINES PER MINUTE
PUNCH	200 CARDS PER MINUTE
MAGNETIC TAPE UNITS	UP TO 34,160 CHARACTERS PER SECOND

The UNIVAC 1005 III System includes magnetic tape storage by the incorporation of UNIVAC VI-C Magnetic Tape Units.

Each of the above models is program compatible with its predecessors, and can be expanded with a wide range of peripheral equipment.

In 49 years, I never got tired of programming because it was always changing. There was always something new: new computers, new operating systems, new programming languages. In the early years I spent all my spare time reading the computer manufacturers' technical manuals, even for computers I never worked on, just because I was so interested in how they all worked.

One day I read an article in Datamation magazine about an ex-UNIVAC Field Engineer who had his own service bureau with a UNIVAC II computer. It was in Gardena, not far from where I was in Lynwood, and my wife was working in an office also in Gardena.

I called her and we met at the place and went inside. The man from the article was there, he greeted us, and he was very pleased to give us a tour. The UNIVAC II computer was so big that it had a door where you could go inside. All three of us were standing upright inside the CPU. I would often say that my mind was inside a computer, but that time my whole body was physically inside one.

While I was working at Western Gear, I took four advanced Computer Science classes at the UCLA Extension. The first one was called Advanced Programming Techniques, and was about IBM OS/360 MVT Internals. MVT is Multiprogramming with a Variable number of Tasks. I knew that the IBM 360 was like the UNIVAC 9400 and that the IBM Disk Operating System (DOS) was like UNIVAC OS/4. So, I just started out with the most advanced class. What I didn't know was that IBM OS was not like IBM DOS at all. I only found out when I got there and then I had to quickly learn all the basic stuff to keep up with the class. The instructor was a Systems Programmer with Security Pacific Bank, and I think all the other students were IBM Systems Programmers too, or at least worked on IBM OS machines. I had a stack of IBM manuals about 3 feet high. The best one, of course, was the classic *IBM 360 Principles of Operation*.

OS/360 was very well designed and very well organized. All the internal data structures are published in IBM manuals. The class was about the internal structures and how to access them by a user program. The final exam was about analyzing a system crash dump. From one fixed location you could find the address of everything else, and therefore diagnose the cause of a crash. Even though I started from far behind the rest of the class, I got an A for the course.

UCLA had what I think must have been one of the biggest computers in the world at that time, about 1970-1971. It was what they called the IBM 360/91 KK. Computer memory then was always measured in thousands (K), so KK stood for a thousand thousand bytes of memory. Now we would say 1 megabyte. One night the class got a tour of the computer room. It was really huge. My probably inaccurate memory of it is that there were large cabinets full of computer equipment for as far as I could see. It was super impressive. We didn't do our class programs there, though. There were remote batch terminals set up around that part of the campus.

File No. S360-01
Form A22-6821-6

 Systems Reference Library

IBM System/360 Principles of Operation

This publication is the machine reference manual for the IBM System/360. It provides a direct, comprehensive description of the system structure; of the arithmetic, logical, branching, status switching, and input/output operations; and of the interruption system.

The reader is assumed to have a basic knowledge of data processing systems and to have read the *IBM System/360 System Summary*, Form A22-6810, which describes the system briefly and discusses the input/output devices available.

For information about the characteristics, functions, and features of a specific System/360 model, use the functional characteristics manual for that model in conjunction with the *IBM System/360 Principles of Operation*. Descriptions of specific input/output devices used with the System/360 appear in separate publications. Publications that relate to the IBM System/360 Model 20 are described in the *IBM System/360 Model 20 Bibliography*, Form A26-3565. Other IBM Systems Reference Library publications concerning the System/360 are identified and described in the *IBM System/360 Bibliography*, Form A22-6822.

An innovation in the Model 91 360 was that it had an instruction pipeline. The execution of an instruction was broken down into maybe 4 or 5 steps, and they could be executed simultaneously. So, the first instruction goes into the pipeline where it executes the first step. Then the first instruction moves on to its second step while the next instruction does its first. The effect is that 4 or 5 instructions can be executing at the same time, which is obviously faster than one at a time. This is not apparent to the Programmer until there is a fault or, in other words, a crash. When that happens there would be a crash dump of the program memory along with the contents of all the program registers including the program counter or PC. The PC has the address of the next instruction, so in a normal computer that's the address after the instruction that had the fault. On the Model 91, the PC had already advanced several instructions. There was no way to know exactly how many because it depended on what the instructions were. That meant the Programmer had to look at as many as 5 instructions back from the PC to find the one that failed. Another unusual thing about the Model 91 was that it did not have decimal arithmetic. Decimal arithmetic instructions were trapped and simulated by software.

In all I took 4 Computer Science courses at the UCLA Extension. My next class was also called Advanced Programming Techniques, but was about IBM OS/360 SYSGEN. Again, this course was for IBM Systems Programmers and again I think I was the only one in the class who was not one. The IBM SYSGEN was based on the MACRO facility of the IBM 360 Assembler Language, the most powerful MACRO facility in the world, in my opinion. The UNIVAC Assembler Language had a similar thing called PROCs, but with nowhere near the capability of IBM MACROs. This class also covered IBM's TSO (Time-Sharing Option), TCAM (Telecommunications Access Method), VS (Virtual Storage) and VM (Virtual Machine).

My third class was called Operating Systems Principles and was about IBM 360 OS and Burroughs 5500 MCP (Master Control Program). There were examples from the Burroughs 5500 computer, but we didn't get to write any programs for that machine. I don't think they even had one. Notable things about that computer were that it had virtual memory before IBM "invented" it for its System 370 computers, and that it was a stack machine. A stack machine meant that it did its operations in reverse Polish order using the stack for operands and results. My fourth class was also called Operating Systems Principles, but was about Compiler Design and Parsing.

I worked at Western Gear from 1970 to 1971. Then something went wrong. I don't know what, but Ron Buffington, the manager who hired me, left. I think he got fired, but maybe he just quit. Then they got a new manager. Sometime after that, a big manager from the main plant came and talked to the staff, and one of the things he said was that if we ever had a problem we could come to his office and tell him about it. I can see you shaking your head already. Never do that!

Well, I had a problem. I wanted to be reimbursed for my classes at UCLA and for some reason I wasn't getting it. I don't think I made a special trip over to the main plant to talk to the big manager, but I don't know why else I would have been there. He was very nice. When I got back, my own manager was furious. I know. I can hear you saying "Ha, ha, I told you so!" He said something about going over his head, and I was gone soon after that.

That sounds bad, doesn't it? Three jobs in three years, and now I was out of work. This time, Ron Buffington didn't get me another job. At least I don't think he did. It came by way of a UNIVAC salesman, and it's possible they knew each other. Actually, I don't know where Ron went. Sadly, I don't think I ever saw or heard from him again. This UNIVAC salesman was regularly visiting a small IBM 360 installation, trying to get them to switch to a newer better UNIVAC computer. He may have also had some personal connection there, like a relative or a friend. Anyway, I didn't know him, but apparently he knew about me. Without ever meeting me, he recommended me for a job there, and they hired me. I don't know, but I think either he just wanted to help a fellow UNIVAC guy, or maybe he thought I would somehow help get them to switch to UNIVAC from the inside. That was never going to happen. They were dedicated to IBM.

CHAPTER 5

1971 - 1972

Management Applied Programming

THE COMPANY WAS called Management Applied Programming (MAP), and was located in Santa Monica. They had an IBM 360 Model 25. It was both the smallest and newest IBM 360 Model. It had 32k bytes of memory and the DOS operating system. We did mostly insurance applications using the IBM Assembler Language and also DYL260. There I met Steen Brydum, by far the smartest and most visionary Programmer I ever met. He was from Denmark.

Steen and I spent hours and hours together trying to make the best possible code, using the IBM Green Card to choose instructions based on their execution times. We also created Macros to do all kinds of things, and I think we were both the most advanced IBM Programmers. We wrote so many Macros that, when we wrote a program using those Macros, it was like coding in our own higher level language.

I was there at MAP from 1971 to 1972. At that time, we still wrote programs with a pencil on programming forms. When a program was finished, we sent it to be keypunched. There was a small group of female keypunch operators who did that and then sent back a deck of cards. Rather than submit the program to be assembled right away, I would send it in for an 80/80 list. That's just a plain listing of the program without any processing at all. MAP had one or two full-time computer operators who ran all the production jobs, and who also ran jobs for the Programmers. They were always busy, so it was faster and easier to get a simple listing of a program.

Now, what do you think I did with the program listing? I debugged the program! In those days, there was no such thing as an interactive debugger. And anyway, I always insisted that a program could and should be debugged just by reading the code. I made corrections with a pencil on the listing and, if there were a lot, I might send it to be keypunched, or, just as likely, I would keypunch the cards myself. Since my first job at GTI, I was very good at keypunching. I might then get another listing, and then check it again to get it to be as correct as I could.

When I thought the program looked ready, I would submit it to be assembled. The Assembler program would turn the source code into object machine code and print a listing with annotations for any errors. It was not really usual to get an error-free assembly the first time, but sometimes I did. More often, I would have to fix at least one line of code, and submit it to be assembled again. My goal was to do this the minimum number of times because the computer was busy, and it could take an hour or so to get a job back. I would be working on more than one program at a time, so I didn't just sit and wait, but still I was always eager to get a program done. Once I got a clean assembly, then I could run a test. Again, it was not usual for me to get a program to work perfectly the first time, but sometimes I did. My old saying: *"More Thought, Less Code"*, was extended to: *"More Thought, Less Debugging"*.

If you're a Programmer now, you would have to disagree with me that any of what I just said was ever possible. Software is much, much larger now, and so complex that a lot of software is never debugged. Since the advent of C++ and Object-Oriented Programming, you really can't even read a program anymore to see what it does. Due to constructors and operator overloading, a simple statement like "a = b + c;" might do anything.

I was with Management Applied Programming for about a year, then I was layed off. I don't think I did anything wrong, maybe it was cutting costs, but they didn't tell me why, so I don't know. However, that year working with Steen Brydum was in my estimation the best experience and training any Programmer could ever possibly get. I can't say that strongly enough.

CHAPTER 6

July - October 1972

Basic / Four Corporation

M Y NEXT JOB was with Basic/Four Corporation in Irvine. Basic/Four created a system based on a Microdata computer with their own Business BASIC language. It was very innovative and very interesting. I did some business applications and technical support. While I was there, I studied the Microdata machine language, which was very interesting in that the instructions were lower level than usual, and considered to be microprogramming. I was only there for a few months, though, from July to October of 1972, when I left for a better job.

For more detailed information, ask for the following
Basic/Four Applications Bulletins:

ORDER ENTRY: Applications Bulletin: BFC 4001

INVOICING/ACCOUNTS RECEIVABLE: Applications Bulletin: BFC 4002

INVENTORY CONTROL: Applications Bulletin: BFC 4003

SALES ANALYSIS: Applications Bulletin: BFC 4009

ACCOUNTS PAYABLE: Applications Bulletin: BFC 4007

PAYROLL: Applications Bulletin: BFC 4006

BFC 4010   JUNE 26, 1972
Copyright© by Basic/Four Corporation. All rights reserved.   Litho USA

Basic/Four is manufactured by the Basic/Four Corporation,
a subsidiary of Management Assistance Inc. (MAI)

All specifications are subject to change without notice.

THE PROGRAMMER

CHAPTER 7

1972 - 1973

Sperry Univac Computer Systems

WHEN I LEFT MAP, it somehow became known in UNIVAC circles that I needed a job. Seemingly out of the blue, I got an offer to work for UNIVAC in the L.A. branch office. I was ecstatic. For me, it was a dream job. In 1972, at 21 years old, I became a UNIVAC Systems Analyst with a salary of $1,000/mo. I don't know what anyone else got paid, but I was very impressed with myself. Systems Analyst was the same job title Ron Buffington had when I first met him. The company was really called Sperry Univac Computer Systems, but it was always UNIVAC to me.

It really was a great job. My office was in a modern office building on Wilshire Blvd., just above their big data center. It was essentially a marketing support job. I had a group of UNIVAC customers who had 9200, 9300 and 9400 computers who could call me if they had any questions or problems. I would be sitting at my desk, and a customer would call and ask me something. I had a set of manuals in front of me from which I would open the right one, find the answer, and tell the customer. If someone had a problem such that I needed to go to their site, I could do that and solve whatever problem they had. It seemed I had full autonomy to do whatever I thought was needed to take care of my customers. I didn't ask permission. I just did it. Customers liked that, and even told me they appreciated my service. I was there from Oct. 1972 to Oct. 1973.

Another thing I did in the marketing area was to set up demonstrations. One time, I was given a program called Optimum Fortran, and was told they would like it to be accessible from a remote terminal at a convention somewhere. It was not written to be an online interactive program. It was my job to make it that way and then to be in the basement computer center to make sure it was working for the demo.

I said before that UNIVAC was big in online real-time systems. Another demo I did involved software that was called the Message Control Program (MCP) and the Information Management System (IMS). What they did was to make a database accessible online from a remote terminal. To get the demo ready, I wrote a COBOL program to read the customer's file from tape and write it into a database on the disk. I invited the customer's data processing manager to be there and help with that process. Then I set it up so that a remote terminal in a conference room there in the building could access the data. The Customers could then see their own data online. I think they liked all that, but I don't remember them actually buying a UNIVAC computer.

What I called a database was an ISAM file, for Indexed Sequential Access Method. This technique was developed by IBM, and they even made it so that their disk controllers could find a record by key all in channel programming. Their disk controllers were connected to the computer by a Selector Channel that had its own instructions. I thought that was all really clever. They didn't need a lot of memory or software to do very sophisticated things. Naturally, I learned all about the disk and tape and other controllers, selector and multiplexor channels, and channel programming. I don't think I got to do channel programming myself, but I knew how it all worked. I also understood ISAM very well, how disks were formatted and how the key indexes were searched. I don't remember if we used the term 'database' back then. Relational databases came much later.

I had another project where I had to convert software from an IBM 360/40 to work on a UNIVAC 9400. The program accessed an ISAM file, and I converted that too. The file format and the access method were different enough that it took a fair amount of work. It just happened that I came to the job already an expert on both the UNIVAC 9400 and the IBM 360. In fact, I was the only one. The 9400 was pretty new, and the people there worked on 9200 and 9300 computers, and the more senior people worked on the UNIVAC 1108. Having a year's experience on the 9400 put me ahead of everyone else, and a year's experience on the 360 made me all that much stronger. Pretty much all the 9400 projects came to me.

When the UNIVAC 9700 came out, I was the one from the L.A. office selected to go to UNIVAC headquarters in Blue Bell, Pennsylvania for the UNIVAC 9700 Startup Workshop. I remember being in a very large computer room that had a UNIVAC 9700, an RCA Spectra 70 and an IBM 360. The RCA computer also copied the IBM 360 instruction set architecture. At that time, UNIVAC had just bought out the RCA computer business. UNIVAC wanted to migrate RCA customers to UNIVAC computers as well as IBM 360 customers. The reason the three machines were in the same room was to demonstrate portability from IBM and RCA to UNIVAC.

In addition to the UNIVAC 9700 Workshop, I had other UNIVAC courses including EXEC 8 Internals, EXEC 8 Panic Dump Analysis, AN-UYK/20 Assembler Language and the CMS-2M programming language, and the Communications Symbiont Processor (C/SP).

Fedco bought a UNIVAC 9480. The 9480 was the same as the 9400 except that it had semiconductor memory instead of plated wire. Where the 9400 had two big cabinets for 131k bytes of memory, the 9480 had just one, and it was half empty. Part of the deal was that we, UNIVAC, would convert all their software from the IBM 360/30 to the UNIVAC 9480. I was in charge of the project from the technical side. My expertise in both systems made it fairly straightforward, but there was still a lot of work. The MCP and IMS systems I mentioned before were an important part of the conversion, but there were some serious problems that made the managers uncomfortable. It eventually got done, and I gave a class to the Fedco staff on the UNIVAC system. The UNIVAC JCL (Job Control Language) was different than IBM's, of course.

Since back to when I was at Management Applied Programming, I had the goal of being able to program every computer in every language. Obviously that's impossible. A life-time is not long enough. At some point much later, I felt that I had achieved that because I had worked

MICHAEL DI LORETO

on so many different computers and in so many different languages that every time I learned a new one it was faster and easier. So, even though I didn't actually program every computer in every language, I was able to. As part of that goal, but also for its own sake, I wanted to work on bigger and bigger computers. UNIVAC's biggest and greatest computer was the UNIVAC 1108. That computer with its EXEC 8 operating system was in my view far ahead of everything else. It was a "true" multiprocessor system. That is, it could have up to three CPU's operating simultaneously with the same memory. The multi-modular memory allowed simultaneous access to different modules. IBM did not have a computer like that. What they called a multiprocessor was two CPU's in a master-slave setup. That's why I emphasized the term 'true' in my description of the 1108.

CHAPTER 8

1973 - 1976

Petersen Publishing Company

I WAS WORKING FOR UNIVAC, but I could not work on the 1108. They had several 1108 experts already and, as I said, I was the leading expert on the 9400. Why would they ever want to move me? No chance. What happened instead was that Petersen Publishing Company in Hollywood bought a UNIVAC 1106 and they needed to hire a programming staff. Someone recommended me, and they offered me a job. Of course, that was exactly what I was dreaming of. When I resigned from UNIVAC, they tried to keep me. I was sent to some office in Century City, I think, to meet some big boss who tried to talk me out of leaving. It was very hard. It really was a great job and I really liked it there. But the UNIVAC 1106 was calling me and I had to go. The 1106 was the same as the 1108, but slowed down to make it cheaper. I think it still cost a million dollars with all the peripherals and so on. I was with Petersen Publishing from 1973 to 1976.

The computer room at Petersen Publishing was the best ever. Not only did it have a raised floor, it was made to look like red carpet. The UNIVAC 1106 had 262k 36-bit words of memory, and the biggest and best maintenance panel ever, with a lot of colorful blinking lights, switches, dials, etc. It was very impressive. IBM didn't make computers like that. The 1106 also had an array of big disk drives, a row of tape drives, a card reader and a big drum printer. The keyboard console was very modernistic. Sitting in front of it was like being in command of a spaceship. There was also a UNIVAC 9300 in the room.

My job was to be a COBOL programmer. I wrote their main application which was the Random File Maintenance program. Petersen Publishing published many magazines. Teen Magazine was the biggest one, but Hot Rod and Motor Trend were also very popular. The Random File Maintenance was run every day to update the subscriptions database. They called it "random" because it accessed the database by key. Non-sequential access was called random access. That was a very big program for that time. It was almost a full box of cards. A box held 2,000 punched cards. Most programs were small enough that you could just put a rubber band around them and carry them in one hand. My program was too big for that, so I carried it around in a box. That sounds funny now, but we carried our programs to the computer room to be compiled, and then carried them back to our offices upstairs. I also wrote the list rental program.

My big goal was to do UNIVAC 1106 Assembler Language programming. In order to learn the language, I invented a play program to simulate the UNIVAC 9300 architecture on the 1106. That is, I used 1106 instructions to execute 9300 instructions. In order to write a program like that, you have to know every instruction on both computers in the finest detail. I even made my program simulate I/O to a tape drive and, in the end, I could put the operating system tape from the 9300 on the 1106 and boot the Tape Operating System. It worked! This took me a long time to do, probably a few months. I just worked on it in my spare time. I still had my real job to do. But I became an expert in everything on the 1106, including the operating system services.

1. INTRODUCTION

A medium-scale extension to the proven UNIVAC 1100 series of computers is provided by the UNIVAC 1106 System. Its modular design provides growth potential within the UNIVAC 1106 as well as possible upgrading to the larger UNIVAC 1108 System.

The UNIVAC 1106 permits the user to select an executive system most applicable to his needs. This selection ranges from EXEC II, which provides a powerful batch processing capability, to the UNIVAC 1106 Executive System with its real-time, multiprogramming, demand, and batch processing ability.

In addition to a versatile executive system, the UNIVAC 1106 utilizes the complete family of UNIVAC 1108 unit processor software, application packages, and peripheral subsystems.

Figure 1-1. The Central Processor and Operator's Console

MICHAEL DI LORETO

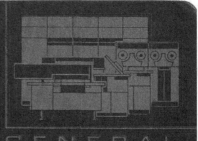

GENERAL
REFERENCE
MANUAL

UNIVAC®

1108

COMPUTER SYSTEM

The UNIVAC 1106, like the 1108, was a 36-bit machine. It had 36-bit registers and the memory was accessed in 36-bit words. It used two different character codes. There was a 6-bit character code called Fieldata and a 9-bit character code called ASCII. There were instructions that could manipulate 6-bit and 9-bit pieces of the registers to deal with characters. The machine used ones-complement arithmetic. Just about every other computer, especially now, uses twos-complement arithmetic. That refers to how negative numbers are represented. In the ones-complement system, a negative number is the binary complement of the positive one. That is, each bit in the negative number is the opposite of the positive one. The funny thing about that was that it made it possible to have a negative zero. To negate a number in the twos-complement system, you complement the number and add one. There is no minus zero.

Part of the deal for Petersen Publishing to buy the UNIVAC 1106 was that they would have three UNIVAC 1100 Systems Analysts on site full time for a year. They set up the operating system and the database, and generally made sure the computer and everything was working okay. There was a time when my manager saw me working on my play program and said something about it, but at the end of the year when the UNIVAC people left, they needed someone to fill that role, and, due to my unauthorized "playing", I was totally qualified for it. I was promoted to Systems Programmer and given a big raise. From then on it was I who did the SYSGEN and maintenance of the EXEC 8 operating system. I also took over the role of Database Administrator. It was a CODASYL database with a Data Definition Language (DDL) and a Data Manipulation Language (DML) that was incorporated into the COBOL language. As Database Administrator, I was responsible for the 3,000,000 subscriber DMS-1100 database, including backup and recovery, schema definition (DDL) and interfacing routines (DML).

On top of everything else, I developed production run procedures in the SSG (Symbolic Stream Generator) Language on the UNIVAC 1106 to help the computer operators run their batch jobs. And I programmed the UNIVAC 1900 CADE (Computer Assisted Data Entry) system in the Data Entry COBOL language. I developed data dictionary and

COBOL copy library generating software in ALGOL, COBOL and Assembler Language on the UNIVAC 1106.

It was not part of my official responsibility, but it happened here as well as in other jobs going back to Western Gear and continuing into the future that I was the one the other Programmers asked for help when they had problems. It did seem to be part of my official duty to help customers, although I don't think it was officially stated anywhere. But somehow the customers knew to call me when they needed help. My personal policy was to always have time to help other people. Throughout my career, whenever anyone asked for help with any problem, I immediately stopped what I was doing and did everything I could to help them. I think I did this naturally, but I was also a member of the ACM (Association for Computing Machinery), which I joined in about 1972 when I was with UNIVAC. The ACM published a code of conduct for computer professionals that, among other things, involved promoting the computer industry by sharing information and generally being helpful to others. Again, I think I would have done that anyway, but I really took the ACM's professional code of conduct to heart.

Here's something interesting. By helping other people, I gained experience from all kinds of problems, more than I would have just by myself. The more I helped other people, the more I learned about various technologies. When someone asked me to help them with something I knew nothing about, I went to work learning about whatever it was to help solve the problem. I think maybe I was unique in this regard. Many Programmers would just say "*I'm busy. Read the manual.*" I was also very busy with my own work, but I would always stop to help others. People liked that, and would always come back to me with problems both simple and very complex.

One time a Customer called me to say the COBOL compiler didn't work. I calmly said "*Okay. Tell me what your program does.*" In just a few minutes on the phone, without ever seeing the program, I could tell him what was wrong and how to fix it. Another time a Customer who was in the office next to the computer room was having trouble with a Fortran program. I happened to be standing nearby and took a look at it. Not even knowing Fortran, I could tell him what was wrong. It did happen, though, that one of my co-worker's COBOL programs didn't work, and on investigating it I discovered that the COBOL compiler really did make a mistake in its generated code. I was able to solve that because when I got the compiler to print the generated code, I could read it and see what was wrong with it, again due to my mastery of the 1106 machine language that I got from working on my play program. I couldn't fix the COBOL compiler, but the problem had to do with a complex logical expression with multiple 'ands' and 'ors', so I helped simplify the code to get around the problem. That solved it.

Sometime in the mid-1970s Structured Programming became a thing. It was a substantial movement, but the most memorable thing had to do with GOTOs. It was also called goto-free programming. GOTO in a program is a statement that jumps to another part of the program. All Assembler Languages have jump or branch instructions, and they're necessary. I don't think there was any proposal to eliminate them. Fortran, COBOL, and Basic all had GOTO statements. I was working in COBOL at the time, so I tried to do Structured Programming in that language. It didn't work out well at all, but it was probably my own fault. I ended up with big pieces of code with no GOTOs, but a lot of if-then-else statements and very deep indentation. I don't know what happened to Structured Programming. I guess it was just a fad that faded out.

I went to see Donald Knuth give a lecture about Structured Programming at UCLA. It was not in a big lecture hall where you needed tickets to get in or anything like you might expect for such a famous person. It was a fairly small lecture room with a stage. It was packed full. There was no standing room. I listened to him from the doorway. The substance of his lecture was his proposal of the COME-FROM statement as a way to eliminate GOTOs. Obviously, it was a hoax.

I don't know if it's right, but it seems to me that so-called algorithmic languages like ALGOL, PL/I, and later C were structured in such a way as to make GOTO's unnecessary. You didn't have to work to get rid of them. They were just not natural. There is a GOTO in C, but you rarely see it. It's even more rare in Object-Oriented languages like C++ and Java.

Another historical thing that I think happened at about the same time was the introduction of the title *Software Engineer*. It started out like a fad, but it kept on going to the point where even people who

MICHAEL DI LORETO

are not in the computer business thought Programmers were Software Engineers. Probably nobody but me calls themselves a Computer Programmer anymore. However, I myself have had titles like Software Engineer, and I've even used that to tell people what I did.

There was always a kind of friendly antipathy between Engineers and Programmers, that is, between hardware and software people. By Engineer, I mean an Electronics Engineer who either designs and builds new electronics devices or services them, like a Field Engineer. It was not uncommon when there was some system problem that software people would blame the hardware and hardware people would blame the software. I personally got along very well with UNIVAC Field Engineers to the point where I could tell them there was something wrong with some hardware and they would believe me. I had that credibility. Later I'll talk about how I used my problem solving technique to find the cause of a failure wherever it was, either in the hardware or in the software, and in what hardware or in what software.

I think what happened was that some Engineer wrote an article saying that engineering was superior to programming because Engineers had a whole catalogue of reliable components that they put together to make new systems. It was very disciplined, whereas programming was all ad hoc and creative, re-inventing everything from scratch, and building flaky systems. If there would only be a catalogue of reliable software components that could be put together to make reliable systems, it would benefit from that engineering discipline, and the people who did that could be called Software Engineers.

I never believed that. I always thought it was just some hardware people criticizing software people for not being as professional as they were. I completely buy whatever Engineers say about their professional discipline, their parts catalogues and tools and all the rest. I also agree that software projects, especially large ones, fail more often than they succeed, and that there are good reasons for that. However, it seems to me that there are plenty of software development tools and libraries of software components. I still don't think that turns a Programmer into an Engineer.

As a member of the ACM, I received their *Communications of the ACM* every month, and as a member of the IEEE Computer Society, I received their magazine *Computer* also every month. They both had articles about Software Engineering, apparently agreeing that it was something.

While I was working for Petersen Publishing I did some moonlighting jobs. One was for Fazio's grocery stores. They had a UNIVAC 1106 and they wanted a program to calculate the distribution of turkeys to their many stores for the upcoming Thanksgiving. I don't know how I got the job. I was probably recommended by some UNIVAC person. They gave me a small machine with a keyboard and printer that I could use to work online on the 1106 from home. I decided to use Fortran for the Thanksgiving Turkey Distribution program mainly to learn Fortran, but also because the program did mathematical calculations that seemed to make it appropriate. It was the first but not the only time I chose a language for a project in order to learn the language. The program was tricky because they wanted to allocate each store a percentage of some total number of turkeys, but turkeys don't naturally divide up that way. Anyway, I finished that job and it must have been okay because they hired me again for the Christmas Turkey Distribution.

Another time, I think it must have been from one of our customers at Petersen Publishing, I was recommended for work on a Data General NOVA minicomputer. It was for a small company in Paramount called WSA Systems and Services. They had a contract with Warner, Electra, Atlantic (WEA) in Burbank to provide Fortran IV programs for their Data General NOVA 840 computer. These were small programs to do various kinds of simple reports. The way it worked was that Warner had a Systems Analyst who wrote very exact specifications for each program and they had a library of subroutines to do most of the common tasks. I would meet with Erwin Warshawsky, the President of WSA, in his office in Paramount. He would give me the specification for a program and I would make an estimate. It would be from about 20 to 40 hours. We would make a fixed-price contract based on my hourly rate of $20/hr, and I would do the job. I would go to the Warner Brothers movie studio in Burbank at night when there was nobody there and work in a small computer room by myself. When the program was done, I would go back to WSA to get paid and then get another one. Erwin said he really liked working with me because I always got the programs done on time. He told me he had several other Programmers doing the same thing, but they mostly didn't get the programs done at all or they took too long. So, I did many of them, and Erwin had a really clever technique. As part of my fixed-price contract for, say, $400, he would add a bonus of maybe another $100 if I got it done by some fixed date, usually within a few weeks. That was very effective. I worked extra hard and I always got that $100.

Then, something really strange happened. That small company and its hole-in-the-wall office got bought out by Data General and became the Data General Systems Division. They had big plans to grow and expand. Erwin offered me a full-time job. This was terrible! I wanted to work on bigger and bigger computers, and here was a job on small minicomputers. It was not the way I wanted to go. On the other hand, I had been with Petersen Publishing for a few years and it was a great job, I was kind of the star of the place, but it was getting too easy. On big computer systems, it seemed like everything was already done. On a minicomputer, everything was still to be invented. Besides that, Data General was now making their Eclipse super-minicomputers, which was a great innovation. I struggled with the decision, then took the job.

CHAPTER 9

1976 - 1977

Data General Systems Division

S O, IN 1976 I was in this small office with second-hand furniture working on Data General computers. The Data General NOVA was the first 16-bit minicomputer. The founders of the company broke off from Digital Equipment Corp. (DEC) where they still had the 12-bit PDP-8. The NOVA instruction set was truly elegant. It was like microprogramming in 16-bit instructions. One instruction could clear a register, do an arithmetic operation, shift the result and skip the next instruction based on some condition all at the same time. Another Programmer and I played with trying to make some code shorter because it just seemed like you could always find a way to take an instruction out. That was David Mapes who at a previous job had the title of *Computer*. He didn't just work on computers, he was one. I think it was because he was a mathematician.

My first project was to develop a Communications Supervisor for a customer of theirs in Las Vegas called Central Credit. Their business was to provide a credit checking service for casinos. They did that with a bunch of people keeping track of gamblers' credit on little slips of paper stuck on several big racks. Now they had bought a Data General Eclipse computer and were automating the process with terminals in the casinos' offices. They had Programmers developing the applications themselves, but I was to provide the software to handle the communications with the terminals. They were connected by leased telephone lines. The Internet was still in the future.

The language of choice on Data General computers was their own version of Fortran IV which was significantly enhanced over the standard version. I made a few short trips to Las Vegas to visit their office, but I did all the work back at my office in Paramount. My Communications Supervisor program handled getting messages back and forth between the terminals and the applications. Data General had a software package called Communications Access Manager (CAM) that did the low level I/O with the communications interface hardware, but I wrote my own replacement package to do the same thing only better. My code supported the Asynchronous Line Multiplexor (ALM), the Synchronous Line Multiplexor (SLM) and the DCU-50 front-end computer. The DCU-50 had the NOVA instruction set, but it was on a separate board from the main computer and the communications interfaces were connected to that. It had direct access to the computer memory to send and receive messages. Lear Seigler ADM-2 terminals were installed in casino offices in Las Vegas in multi-drop configurations. That is, several terminals were connected to the same phone line and the software selected the one to send and receive messages by polling. Each terminal on the line had a different address so that they wouldn't conflict with each other. They also had a NOVA 830 in Reno that acted as a remote concentrator. The terminals used asynchronous communications, but the communications between the two computers was synchronous with a binary synchronous protocol which I modeled after IBM's Bisync.

Data General's Real-Time Disk Operating System (RDOS) had a way to do I/O and handle interrupts from a user device driver. It was way better and easier than other systems where you had to do complicated things to install a device driver that had to run in supervisor mode.

RDOS
REAL TIME
DISK OPERATING SYSTEM
USER'S MANUAL

DATA GENERAL
CORPORATION

093-000075-04

MICHAEL DI LORETO

ECLIPSE® C/350
Principles of Operation

Data General

The Data General Systems Division needed much bigger and better offices. They bought a very nice building in Anaheim not far from Disneyland and we all moved there. It was close enough that I sometimes went to Disneyland for lunch. They won a big contract from the L.A. Times. They hired new additional managers and staff. It was not easy to find experienced Data General Programmers, so they got people from other types of computers. They wanted to hire 14 Programmers for that contract, but were never able to do so. The job they wanted to do was similar to what I had done for Central Credit, and I thought I could do the whole project myself, or maybe with another good Programmer from our old office. I considered this a classic case of a failed software project. The project manager actually had a copy of *The Mythical Man-Month* on his desk. It's an old book, but if you're a Programmer, you need to read it. It's about the development of IBM's OS/360. Even if you haven't read it, the title gives it all away. You're probably even on a project right now that has been estimated in man-months and the managers think that hiring more people can get the job done faster. That book was first published in 1975, and I had already read it long before seeing it on that manager's desk. But I didn't have to read it to know that the way they were doing the project was wrong. I was there from June of 1976 to October of 1977.

While I was there, I wrote a multi-tasking executive for the Data General microNova. The microNova was the first 16-bit microprocessor. Bigger Data General computers had an operating system called RDOS (Real-Time Disk Operating System). It was one of the few true real-time operating systems. The other one I knew was UNIVAC EXEC 8. My definition of "real-time" is a system with an interrupt-driven priority scheduler. EXEC 8 actually had three schedulers: batch, timesharing and real-time. I was serious when I said "few". IBM operating systems, OS and DOS, were not real-time. Neither was DEC VMS nor Microsoft Windows. There are real-time applications running on those systems. If the computer is fast enough, you can get away with it.

Debbie Runner had been a Programmer sitting at the desk next to mine in Paramount. Now she was the manager of her own group in Anaheim. They were doing a project on the microNova, and instead of using the RTOS provided by Data General, she decided to use my multi-tasking executive with its own downline loading because it used less memory and had less system overhead. My play program became part of a real project.

CHAPTER 10

1977 - 1978

Sperry Univac Computer Systems

I WAS KIND OF dissatisfied with the way things were there, so, in 1977, when UNIVAC offered me a job, I took it. I became a Data Processing Consultant on site at California Federal Savings in L.A. The Data Processing Consultant title was higher than Senior Systems Analyst which was higher than Systems Analyst, which I had been several years before. It was a big project. There were a lot of people both from CalFed and from UNIVAC. They were upgrading their systems from a UNIVAC 492 computer to a new UNIVAC 1100/82 system. My part was to develop the Optional Database Service (ODS) for the TIP COBOL interface to DMS-1100. TIP was their Transaction Interface Package. They used that to process transactions from remote terminals in COBOL. I mentioned before that you could write DML right in a COBOL program, but they had determined that that was too complicated for every application to do, so they wanted to centralize database access code in one place. Their Systems Designers seemed to be very good.

When I was with UNIVAC before in the L.A. branch office, one of my tasks for a Customer was to manually create decision tables on decision table forms. I don't know if I did a particularly good job of it. It was just on paper. It didn't really do anything. But I learned a lot about decision tables and, besides reading computer manuals all the time, I was also reading any published computer books I could get. I had a set of books just about decision tables.

The task I was assigned to do for CalFed seemed to me to be a perfect case for decision tables. The software could be in some state and some input would arrive that would make it do some action and then go to another state. I was able to write down all the states and all the actions and draw the whole thing in one big table. I decided to implement the software that way. I used the UNIVAC 1100 Assembler Language PROC facility to write macros to describe all the states and actions, and then I implemented the whole decision table with it. The main benefit of a decision table is that you can see at a glance what the actions are for every combination of input and state. It looks like a matrix and any cell that's not filled in is obvious. What I wanted to do was to invent a high-level language that would be human-readable the way that a paper decision table was, but also be machine readable. This actually worked. I implemented the whole database interface that way. One time, I printed it and showed it to one of the Analysts, and, seemingly impressed, he said he was really surprised that that was even possible.

I have a thing about software that's probably going to sound kind of weird, but I hope my explanation makes sense. Remember what I said about the Analyst, the Programmer and the Computer. Sounds like a fable, doesn't it? Well, the Analyst writes specifications in English and gives them to the Programmer. The Programmer reads the specifications and then writes a program in code for the computer. Then the computer reads the code and does what it says. Finally, the results go back to the Customer to see if they match what they were expected to be. Sometimes they are, sometimes not. I see this as a communications problem, similar to the old game where one person tells another person something, that person tells a third person the same thing, and so on for several people until the last one says it out loud to compare with the original message, which is funny to see how much the message has changed. When the Analyst gives the specifications to the Programmer, they may in places be incorrect, incomplete or misunderstood. The Programmer codes what he thinks is right, but then here and there makes mistakes or omissions. The computer does exactly what it's told. The very worst thing you can hear from the Customer when he sees the results of months or years of work is: *"That's not what I meant."* Here's my idea of how to fix that. I understand it's not always possible.

Make a way to write specifications so that they are both human-readable and can be executed by the computer. You may have seen references to executable specifications in the literature, but they are mostly hypothetical. My technique was to do that for real. The way I did it was essentially to design a specification language that's human-oriented, but at the same time is written according to fixed rules that can be programmed into a computer. I sometimes called it a language for programming an application. My theory is that most any program can be divided into two distinct parts. One part is to do what the application is intended to do. The other part is all the things you have to do make the program work. I also think that, generally, the code that's needed just to make a program work can be much larger than the code that actually does the application functions. So, you build an infrastructure that includes the things to make the program work, and then write the relatively small application-specific code in a language that's interpreted by that structure. I've proven that this technique works many times on many different systems. I don't do it for every application, but for the ones where I have done it, the results were great. Besides that, and maybe even more importantly, even without inventing a new language, just dividing a program into those two types of code will give you a much better program. It may not be human-readable in the way I just described, but it will have some of the other benefits of being easier to maintain and easier to understand. Programs always change. You should plan on it. When you inevitably make a change, this type of organization of the code will make it more reliable and less likely you'll break something. It will also be easier to understand both by you and by other Programmers coming after you. My saying: *"If you don't understand it, you can't make it work."*

CalFed had a UNIVAC 492 computer. That was exciting to me. The UNIVAC 490 was advertised as the world's first commercial real-time system. It was used by banks like CalFed to support a network of teller terminals in branch offices. It had a feature they called Externally Specified Indexing (ESI). What that did was to set up the communications interface hardware to store messages directly into memory, unlike even later systems that had an interrupt for every character. The 492 was a newer model of the 490 series. The Assembler Language was called SPURT (Systems Programming Under Real-Time). The name of the operating system was REX for Real-Time eXecutive.

I wrote a simulator of the UNIVAC 492 instruction set using the Assembler Language on the UNIVAC 1106. As I said before, you really have to know all the instructions for both machines in very fine detail to do that. I also wrote some small play programs for the real UNIVAC 492.

| UP-4067 | **UNIVAC 491/492**
CENTRAL PROCESSOR | Rev. 1 | 2
SECTION: | 1
PAGE: |

Figure 2–1. The UNIVAC 491 and 492 Real-Time System

2. INTRODUCTION

The UNIVAC 491 and 492 Real-Time Systems are large scale, solid state, general purpose digital computing systems which efficiently satisfy the combined requirements of online and batch processing. Concurrent execution of real time program elements are balanced with execution of program elements for which time is not critical, in order to achieve this optimum efficiency. Non-critical elements operate within a priority structure and are interrupted for processing of critical-priority program elements. The essential difference between the two systems is that the UNIVAC 491 Real-Time System has 8 input/output (I/O) channels; the UNIVAC 492 Real-Time System, 14 I/O channels. A complete system is shown, in block diagram in Figure 2–2.

A. CENTRAL PROCESSOR

The central processor has the following capabilities:

■ Compatibility with a complete family of standard peripheral devices and communication subsystems.

■ Multiplexing on the communication subsystems, permitting random interleaving of data to and from different I/O devices which may be located on site or at a remote site.

■ Compatibility with UNIVAC 490 programs.

■ Facilities for interconnection of one or two on-site central processors.

■ Random access memory with minimum capacity of 16,387 (16K) 30-bit words, expandable in increments, to 65,536 (65K), with 4.8-microsecond cycle time.

■ Seven uniquely addressable index registers for effective addressing.

■ Time orientation to a 24-hour day clock, permitting processing operations to be conditioned by the time of day, and to a real time clock and interval timer to prevent program looping and for time analysis of central processor operation.

■ Programmed write protection preventing a program from affecting elements of unrelated programs.

THE PROGRAMMER

While I was working at CalFed, I did some other outside contract jobs. Dave Mapes, the Programmer I played take-out-one-more-instruction with at our original Data General office, went on to work with another guy named Ron Mur who was an electronics engineer. Their company was called ROM Systems, Inc. They designed a Microprogrammable Data Processor, ROM I, they wanted to sell as a controller for something. Dave was going to do the programming. This was a new computer with a new microcode instruction set that they had just invented, and they needed a Cross Assembler for it. They hired me to write one for them. They had an IBM 360/30 in their office to run it on. I did it for a price fixed at $20/hr for 40 hours, or $800. For my information, they had a printed description of the machine, and for the source language Dave wrote down all the instruction and operand combinations by hand on a piece of paper. These were my requirements or specifications or whatever. Think about what I said about that. How likely would it be there was going to turn out to be something off or missing that would have to be fixed later?

I spent a lot of time designing a specification language to describe the source code formats and options and the object code formats. The microcode had 32-bit long instruction words that could do many things at one time. I used 360 Assembler MACROs to implement my language, different MACROs for the source code and the object code. This was going to be a pretty standard two-pass Assembler that allowed forward references to labels and generated an assembly listing. I want to go back to my theory of dividing a program into two parts, an application-specific part and a part that makes the program work. Using my example just now, you can imagine an Assembler program that reads input source code, makes a label table, generates object code and prints a listing without ever thinking about what the source code or the object code are. All that is the working part, and can be thought of as kind of generic. The application-specific part in this case is the actual format of the source code and the object code. It doesn't matter what they are, the assembly process is the same.

The MACROs I designed made it look like there was one line for each source code format, intentionally very similar to what Dave had written by hand, and one line for each object code format according to the manual. That is, it was not very long. It took maybe three or four printed pages altogether. I could show this to Dave and he could instantly read and understand what it said. He could also see a few mistakes, either that he made when he first wrote it down, or that I made, and the changes were trivial and reliable. They liked it and I got paid. Frankly, I might have gone a little bit over my 40 hours. I didn't keep track of the time. And it's hard to justify, isn't it? There's very little time, so the natural inclination is to just write the code in the most straightforward way possible. Taking the time to invent a new language and then implementing it seems like a very long detour. However, I would maintain that putting extra time into the front end will save even more time at the end. Just think about how my customer, Dave, could see mistakes in my formal specification language and make easy corrections before ever using the program. What if those same mistakes were buried in a big Assembler Language program? They would probably not be found until he was actually using the program and it did something wrong.

For further vindication, a few years later they built another Microprogrammable Data Processor, ROM II, this time a 48-bit one, and they needed another Cross Assembler. They called me and I estimated 20 hours, or $400. Using the same code from my first Cross Assembler, I used the same MACROs to describe the new source and object code formats. I had to make some small change to the underlying code, but that was it. It just worked right away.

I want to point out that, for these two Cross Assemblers and for my Decision Table Processor at CalFed, the final implementation of the programs was declarative. That means the lines of code state what is, not what to do. There are no steps, no procedures, no loops or algorithms. There is an ancient debate about whether any non-trivial program can ever be reliable. I would say that, yes, they can, if they're coded as declarative statements without steps, procedures, loops or algorithms. I'll show examples later of similar techniques that do use steps, but are easily human-readable and reliable.

At the same time as doing my full-time job on the UNIVAC computer at CalFed and on the IBM computer at the little microcontroller company,

I had another part-time job at Management Applied Programming with my old friend Steen Brydum. They had a newer bigger office on Wilshire Blvd and Steen was now the Vice President. They had an IBM 360/65 with OS/MVT, and they were converting their applications from DOS. Steen had the vision of creating an automatic DOS-to-OS conversion system. When he told people about his plan they said it was impossible. He asked them why. When they told him, he worked on the problem until it was solved, and then did it again. When people finally stopped telling him it was impossible, he decided to build it. Three of us developed the automatic DOS-to-OS conversion system that converted Assembler, COBOL and DYL260 programs and produced completely operational OS JCL.

For my part, I decided to use PL/I because, again, I didn't know it. I claim it was appropriate because there was a lot of string manipulation involved in, for example, reading a DOS COBOL program and automatically rewriting it for OS. PL/I has good features for doing that. If it weren't for Steen's plan, I probably would have said it was too big a job and maybe even impossible. But he really did think of everything and we spent several months working together at night to do it. I didn't create a new language for this project. For one thing, it was Steen's project and I was just following his plan. And I probably wouldn't have been able to do it myself. Only Steen Brydum had the powerful vision and the super technical ability to even attempt such a thing.

It was the only time I ever worked on three different jobs at the same time, and it was on three different kinds of computers and in three different languages. But I was just about done with all of them. By coincidence, just at that time, I got a call from Dave Mapes recommending me for a contract job with Infodetics in Anaheim. They made a Document Storage and Retrieval System that was a big mechanical device controlled by a Data General NOVA 3 computer.

CHAPTER 11

1978 - 1979

Infodetics, Corp.

A DOCUMENT FOR INFODETICS was a microphotograph of an engineering drawing mounted on a punched card. The punch card identified the contents of the drawing. The machine had cartridges that would hold 100 cards each, and there were racks that would hold some large number of the cartridges. The machine had a servo mechanism that went up and down and back and forth and could pick a cartridge off a rack and then pick a card out of the cartridge. The machine could then put the card in front of a remote viewer for a person to look at. There was a card reader, also controlled by the computer, that could feed cards into the machine to be put into a cartridge and put away on a rack. There was another machine that could duplicate the cards.

The Infodetics system had a big disk drive where they wanted to keep all the information about the cards, so the computer could know where to get and put the cards in the storage machine. They wanted me to make a database for all that information. It would be a full-time contract job. I'd done many contract jobs before, but always part-time while I had a full-time job. Now, I would have to quit my job with UNIVAC and become a full-time Independent Consultant. That seemed kind of risky, not having an employer and working for myself, but I went for it. They gave me an office there at Infodetics, and I designed the software to manage their database. Remember I said that one of my reasons for going to work on minicomputers was that on big computers everything was already done? Well, Data General didn't provide any database management software. I don't think they even provided big multi-platter disk drives like the ones on big computers. That gave me the opportunity to design my own database system from scratch, and not just for play. I was getting paid a pretty good hourly rate. I don't remember now, but I think it was better than my old $20/hr. My design followed the Indexed Sequential Access Method (ISAM) I learned from IBM. That is, the idea of keyed access to multiple levels of indexes was similar. The software design and all the implementation were entirely my own.

The Infodetics machines were all new. The engineers were there designing and building them in the same big building. When I was finished with the database, other Programmers were still trying to program the other machines. One guy I remember worked on the card reader for a long time and never got anywhere near done. He left, and it fell to me to take it over. Working with another Programmer named Phil McCauley, together we came up with the idea of creating a language for controlling the mechanical machines and a simulator for interpreting it. The language looked like an Assembler Language, and the instructions were implemented using Data General Assembler Language MACROs. Although the system was conceived by both of us together, I think I wrote all the code. I was the one who had written simulators for other computers' instruction sets twice before, two of my play programs. I was the one who had already done lots of language creation using Assembler Language MACROs. And I was the one who, by intimately knowing many computers' different instruction sets, was capable of creating an entirely new one. I called it a hypothetical distributed multiprocessor because it could coordinate several parallel I/O control processes. I can't take all the credit because Phil really did help get it started.

The instructions of my hypothetical computer were like low level machine instructions, but they were intended for controlling external mechanical devices. It was a language for writing device drivers. My inspiration, of course, was from the old Burroughs TC-500 Macro Assembler Language which also had 16-bit instructions for their special purpose. I once made a point about using all my experience on computers no one had ever heard of, and this is a perfect example of that. This was about 10 years later, but I still had ideas from the TC-500 in my head.

I designed the Infodetics 410 I/O computer architecture and implemented the Simulator and Programming Language in Data General NOVA Assembler Language. This hypothetical distributed multiprocessor provided for the coordination of many parallel I/O control processes and a very high level of programmability. Then I developed Working Modules (distributed multi-threaded device drivers) in the 410 I/O computer pseudo Assembler Language for the Autofile, Notcher, Card Selector, TV Zoom Scan and Card-to-card Duplicator.

When I say "multi-tasking", I mean separately scheduled flows of control within a program. When I say "multi-threaded", I mean multiple tasks executing the same code. Multi-threaded code has to be reentrant, whereas separate tasks don't necessarily have to be. When Sun invented *Threads* in the early 1980s, they meant what I call multi-tasking.

In order to store a document in the Infodetics document storage and retrieval system, the card the document is on is first read by the Autofile (card reader). Then notches are made in the card by the Notcher. Then the card is put into a cartridge by the Card Selector. Finally, the cartridge is put away on one of the racks (storage). The notches in the card are the means by which the Card Selector picks a card out of a cartridge (retrieval). Then the card moves to the TV Zoom Scan.

These devices can be operated independently and in parallel. That is, after reading one card it goes from the Autofile to the Notcher. At the same time, another card may be read. Then when the first card moves from the Notcher to the Card Selector, the second card can move from the Autofile to the Notcher, and a third card can be read. This kind of a pipeline is faster overall than moving a card through the whole system before reading another card. The naïve way to program a system like that would be to process the cards one at a time in series. My design allowed it to be done in parallel, all the devices operating at once.

The way I structured that was for each device driver to be a separate task. For example, when the Autofile task was finished reading a card, it would fork another task for the Notcher. You might see that term, 'fork', in the literature, referring to starting another flow of control, but in my pseudo computer architecture, that was a machine instruction. Maybe you can imagine the complexity of the underlying code needed to make that one instruction work. For me, though, having worked on so many real-time systems before, it was not hard to do.

With the instruction set defined and the simulator written, I could then write a device driver for the card reader, called the Autofile. It was maybe two pages long and, with everything else working, it was pretty fast to implement and test. I want to repeat what I said about taking the long detour of designing and implementing a new language to come all the way around to coding the final application. It took a fair amount of time to do all that preparatory work, but when it came to what it was all for, it was fun. I think the guy that was working on it before took more time and didn't finish. Somebody else wrote the code for the servo machine, so I didn't do that. But when the engineers came up with new machines, like the Notcher, Card Selector, TV Zoom Scan and the Card-to-card Duplicator, they told me how it worked, and I wrote the driver for it that day. All that foundational work which seemed like going way out of the way for the first implementation looks a lot better when you get the second, third, fourth and fifth ones almost free.

The Document Storage and Retrieval System could hold a very large number of documents, but it was finite. They wanted to expand the capacity, so they bought two more Data General NOVA 3 computers to control second and third document storage and retrieval machines. But they didn't want completely separate systems because there was one database. It just happened, as you may recall, that I was an expert in computer to computer communications, especially on Data General computers. I connected them together with RS-232 cables for full duplex asynchronous communication, and wrote software to make them work in a master/slave arrangement. There was still one database on the master computer, but it could send messages to the slave computers to store and retrieve documents there. I wrote a formal paper as a kind of tutorial in asynchronous communications and presented it to the staff at an internal seminar.

At Infodetics, I worked with Martin Orton. He was from England and a little older than me, with even more experience, and I always looked up to him. He had been working at the NASA Jet Propulsion Laboratory (JPL) in Pasadena for many years, but now he had gone off to be an Independent Consultant like I did. At the end of our time there, he went back to JPL as a contractor. I didn't have a good job for awhile. I did some contract work installing communications software that I had written for Data General computers for a couple of different small companies. My old friend and colleague from Data General, Debbie Runner, had become the manager of a software group at TRW Validata in Anaheim. She hired me for a part-time contract there.

CHAPTER 12

February - March 1979

TRW Validata

VALIDATA WAS A small part of TRW that did online credit checking for credit cards in airports. It was located in the basement of a big TRW building. They had an old Data General NOVA with operating system software that they had written themselves. Debbie was in charge of a project to upgrade to a new NOVA 3 computer with standard Data General software. The staff there was converting their programs to work on the new machine. The communications interface hardware was a thing they had built themselves called an ASCII board. Naturally, on the new computer they wanted to use Data General communications hardware, and I happened to be an expert in that. Debbie knew that, and assigned me to do their communications work.

Upstairs, TRW had an Amdahl 470V/6 computer that we in Validata used to compile programs. That was strange, but their programs were still on punched cards and that was what we had to do. To me, that meant to get an assembly I had to submit a job to the 470 and wait for the results to come back. To do my job, I had a little familiarity with their old home-grown operating system. Other than that, I'm not sure why, though, it seemed like I had some spare time.

One day they had a weekly staff meeting. I had never been to one before, but this time, since I wasn't doing much, I sat in. They went around the table talking about whatever they were doing, and then they were done. At the end, the big manager, Debbie's superior, asked her how it was going with some problem they'd apparently been having for some time. She told him it was still the same. Their system was live

24/7 except for a short time in the middle of the night when they made a backup copy of their big disk. The problem was the copy program was failing intermittently, causing the operator to have to run it again, sometimes more than once. Their chief Programmer who had written their operating system no longer worked there, but he had been coming back at night to try to solve that problem. I don't know how often. I don't think it was every night. But this had been going on for several months and was very serious.

After the meeting, Debbie and I were alone in the meeting room just getting up to leave after everyone else, and I had heard her and the higher manager talking about this problem. So, I told her something like, "*You know, I can sometimes fix things like that. Can I take a look at it?*" She looked at me like she was about to say, "*What? Are you kidding?*", but then remembered it was me, and said, "*Okay.*" I've mentioned how I solved problems for other people many times over the years. That was all just knowledge and experience, and an interest in solving problems. But I had a theory about it. I called it my famous, patented two-step problem solving technique. Of course, it was neither famous nor patented. I just say that to mock myself. What was so advanced about my two-step process was that everyone else seemed to approach problems with just one: guess what's wrong and change it to see if the problem goes away. My much more advanced technique, mocking again, was first gather up all the relevant information, then solve the problem.

So, I got all the information I could, which included a printed copy of the copy program, the manual for the disk drive and controller, a printed copy of the disk driver software, and a printed copy of their operating system, which I already had because I had looked at it before. I took all that into another small room and started reading. I read through the copy program which was pretty short. I read the disk controller manual. I looked through the listing of the disk controller software. I kind of randomly glanced through the operating system code. Then, I noticed that the guy that was working on it at night had written the contents of the registers after the crash on the back of one of the listings. The Data General NOVA had four 16-bit registers they called accumulators, and they could be displayed in lights on the front panel one at a time using switches that were there. The lights normally displayed the program counter (PC), and a frequent way a Data General program crashed had it end up executing at location zero, which made the next instruction location one. The contents of location zero was zero, which when executed meant jump to location zero. That put the machine in a hard loop executing that one instruction forever.

The PC value of one was of no use. That was normal for a crash. The contents of the accumulators were not definitive at all. I just went through the listings looking for anything that might correspond to the four values. When I was looking through the listing for the disk driver software, I came to a page of code where some of the values could possibly match. That page had a comment title that said CRC error handling. Then I got excited. I knew exactly what that was.

A CRC, or Cyclic Redundancy Check, is used to detect errors in disk records. It's like a parity check but more complex. The CRC is calculated by the disk controller and appended to every record written on the disk, and then when the record is read it's calculated again and compared to the value that was written. If different, it means the data is wrong. This usually happened when there was something wrong with the disk itself. The magnetic disks in those days were imperfect. I experienced this when I was with UNIVAC the first time. There can be bad spots on the disk. When the software runs into one, it has a way to mark it as bad, and there are spare tracks on the disk that can be used instead. A bad spot on the disk is not always all bad. When there is a CRC error reading a record from the disk, the way to handle it is to try again. CRC errors are *intermittent* errors. The reason that excited me was that I was looking for an *intermittent* problem. When the copy failed, they tried it again, and it could work.

The values in the accumulators took me to a page of code for the CRC error handling routine, but that's all. So, I had to look at every instruction one by one to see if I could see anything wrong, also referring to the contents of the accumulators in case there was any clue. The assembly listing had the source code and the generated object code. About halfway down the page, I noticed something strange about the object code for one of the instructions. I never memorized all the binary codes, but I could tell this one didn't look right. It was a jump to the address in location one. At location one there was a zero, which meant jump to location zero, and you're dead!

To see how it got that way, I had to look at the source instruction very carefully. It was supposed to be "jmp @.+1". That means jump to the code whose location is in memory at the next location after the current instruction. The "." means the current instruction address, so ".+1" means the next address after that. The "@" is for indirect. That means jump to the address that's *at* that address. It was a little hard to tell, but what the code actually said was "jmp @,+1". What that means is jump to the address at location one, whose effect is to jump to location zero and die.

This all took less than an hour. I packed up everything to go and show Debbie, and it was so soon that she was still in conversation with her manager at the water cooler. When I came up to her and told her I found what's wrong, she looked at me again, like, "*What? Are you kidding?*" and then again remembered it was me and looked to see what I had. She had been a good Data General Programmer herself, and all I had to do was tell her about the comma where there was supposed to be a period, and she immediately knew what that meant. She literally ran into the computer room to get the box of cards with the disk driver software and found the card with the bad instruction. She looked at it carefully and could see that there really was a comma there. Problem solved. I think I earned my $20 that day.

When I solve a problem, I want to resolve every loose end. First, I found out that the disk driver software had been delivered to them as a listing, and they had keypunched it there in their office. It was a keypunch error. Now, keypunch machines had a verify mode where you put in cards that were already punched and, if you punch the same thing again it's okay, and if not you're stopped. This verification is normally done by a different keypunch operator. That process is not foolproof, and they missed it this time, I guess because the listing was not clear. Then, why was it so hard to see the code was wrong on the assembly listing? It was because they used a drum printer, which I was very familiar with from UNIVAC drum printers as not printing as clearly as, say, an IBM 1403 printer, which, with its print chain, was the gold standard in computer printing.

And, why didn't the Assembler notice that the source code was incorrect? Having written lots of parsing code, I know how difficult it is to get it right. It's such a common thing it shouldn't be that hard, but it can be very tricky. A comma is mostly used just as a separator, like white space, so some parsers just skip over them. In this case it would make the code look like "jmp @+1". Now, you wouldn't write a plus sign with a positive number, but it's not really wrong, just meaningless. It's as if it said "jmp @1" which, of course, is fatal.

But why were the disks getting errors in the first place? I didn't know this in advance, but what happened was that an operator had put a sticky label on a disk, and the disk spinning very fast, I think something like 4800 RPM, the label flew off and gummed up the read/write heads which then in turn corrupted the disk. I didn't get the whole story, but it has happened that the next step was to put the corrupted disk in another disk drive which then messes up those read/write heads too, then put in another disk which also gets corrupted until eventually all the disks and all the disk drives are screwed up. I don't know how far that got in this case, but after they replaced all the heads and cleaned all the disks, the problem started happening, an obvious clue.

I never met the guy who was working nights for several months, so I have no way to explain why he didn't do the same thing I did. It seems pretty obvious now, doesn't it? It happened to me from time to time that I would solve some monumental problem and the manager would then have an attitude like, "*Well, of course, exactly what anyone would have done.*" Usually, there was no way to compare to what anyone would have done, but a few times it happened like this. Someone was working on a problem for several months and didn't solve it, and then I fixed it right away. This was not the only time. It reminds me of Sherlock Holmes.

I was a big fan of Sherlock Holmes and I think I've seen just about every movie and TV series multiple times. Besides just enjoying the stories, I thought we had a lot in common. I thought of myself as a computer detective, using pure deductive reasoning to solve difficult problems. Sometimes I thought of myself as a computer janitor too, cleaning up software messes. It often happened to Sherlock Holmes that, after explaining how he deduced something, some uneducated person would say to him something like, "*Oh, I thought that was really something, but now that you explained it, I can see it was nothing at all.*" That's what happened to me sometimes, "*Oh, sure, that's just what anyone would have done.*"

Sherlock Holmes told Dr. Watson, "*I never guess.*" It wasn't true. He guessed all the time and was often wrong. I didn't think I was imitating him, but I had a similar attitude. I mentioned it before when I said my two-step method was better than just taking a guess. It was kind of funny when someone asked me to help them find out why their program didn't work and I would sit next to them to see what it was. They would immediately start talking real fast about what they thought was wrong, which could be the computer or the compiler or someone else's code. Over and over again, I found myself saying, "*Slow down. Tell me what this does.*" And as often as not, when they did that they found their own error, thanked me and took off. And as I was saying, I wanted everything to be explained, no loose ends. The problem going away was not good enough. I had to know what really caused the problem and why the code change really fixed it. I was very strict with myself about that. Maybe you know about the *printf* fix. I'll explain it later.

Sherlock Holmes also said: "*When you have eliminated the impossible, whatever remains, however improbable, must be the truth.*" Wrong. That doesn't allow for anything to be unknown. Of course, in a detective story, you're supposed to know all the clues and suspects so you can try to solve the mystery along with the great detective. In real life, though, the cause of a problem may be something you didn't even know exists. It seems to be human nature to use logic like, "*It must be this because it can't be anything else.*" You've heard this. It happens all the time with computer software. It's basically the one-step problem solving technique I keep mocking. Using my two-step technique, I go to where the problem is wherever it is. It's good to prefer to look at your own code first, and especially at whatever you changed last. And it's usually a mistake to guess that something else like the compiler is causing your problem. I told you about a case where I actually did find the compiler was wrong, but it's really rare. I even solved a problem one time on a computer with four CPU's where one of them had a defect that caused random failures.

About this same time, I had several very interesting contract jobs. My friend from Basic/Four, Dave Cooper, and I developed a small operating system in Assembler Language for a Computer Automation LSI 2/20 minicomputer at the Arcadia Police Department.

I wrote an inventory control program in DataBasic on a Microdata Reality System for Kirk Paper Company in Commerce, CA.

I wrote master file update and report programs in the IBM 3741 Assembler Language for the American Can Company in Glendale, CA. When I went there, a girl in the office would say, *"It's the computer man."* I kind of liked that. *The Computer Man.*

I wrote a batch order entry program in RPG-II on a Burroughs B-700 computer for Sonic Wire Corporation in Encino, CA.

I developed a subscription fulfillment system on a UNIVAC 1050 in Assembler Language for Neasi-Weber and Associates in Hollywood. Dennis Neasi was the manager who hired me at Petersen Publishing Company. That's another manager who hired me twice. Of all the different computer architectures I've known, the UNIVAC 1050 was maybe the strangest. There were instructions like LP (logical product) and LS (logical sum). If you know Boolean logic, you can probably guess that a logical product is an "and" and a logical sum is an "or". It had 6-bit bytes, which they called "characters", and groups of 4 of them that we would normally call "words", they called "tetrads". It had a teletype for a console.

UNIVAC® 1050 SYSTEMS

THE
CENTRAL PROCESSOR
MODEL IV

The Central Processor Model IV is available for organizations that have unusually fast throughput requirements, and for Model III Processor users who may desire to expand. Complete program compatibility with Model III programs is provided. The minimum specifications of the Model IV Central Processor with the available options are as follows:

- 8192 Character Core Memory– Basic
- 2 Microsecond Cycle Time Per 2 Characters
- Maximum Channel Buffering
- Complete Channel Overlap
- Individual Distinct Channel Interrupts
- 7 Index Registers
- 2 Arithmetic Registers
- Powerful Instruction Logic
  - variable field lengths 1 to 16 characters
  - mass memory move 1 to 1024 characters
  - single character/constant commands
  - hi-lo-equal compare
  - binary/Decimal add and subtract
  - add and subtract to or from memory or register

- unique code translation command
- powerful edit commands
- full suppression commands
- zero and comma suppress
- zero and comma suppress with asterisk fill
- zero and comma suppress with floating $ sign
- Complete Parity Checking
- Integrated Console

OPTIONAL FEATURES
- 8192 Character Plug-in Incremental Memory to 65K of Memory
- Advanced Logic 1 Decimal Multiply and Divide
- 8 Input/Output Channels
- Freestanding Console

CHAPTER 13

March - June 1979

Ford Aerospace

I HAD A BIGGER contract with Aeronutronic Ford in Irvine, part of Ford Aerospace. The job was to develop a Real-Time Data Acquisition and Display system for their DIVAD tank project. Its purpose was to test a new tank they were building for the U.S. Army. They were using a Data General computer with RDOS, the best real-time system, in my opinion. The project was organized as what they called a Skunk Works. I don't think they invented the term, but they seemed to take it seriously. There was a manager and four contract Programmers. That's all. The idea of the Skunk Works was do to the job very quickly by eliminating bureaucracy and red tape. This actually worked. The job was done very fast. I agree with it because my best jobs were all done with either a very small group of people or just by myself. My part was the real-time executive, mag tape recording, oscillograph display task and system integration.

The software project ended in just a few months, but I was not out of work. Ford kept me on at their facility in Newport Beach. It was good to get paid, but it wasn't really a software job. It seemed like their business was in making proposals to the U.S. Government and trying to get big contracts from them. The proposal I helped develop was something pretty much impossible for the technology of the time, 1979. I didn't stay there long.

My friend Martin Orton who I worked with at Infodetics went back to JPL in Pasadena. He arranged for me to go there for an interview with a manager he knew. I had invested in a resumé that was professionally printed and bound, and I took it with me. When I met the manager I gave him the resumé and he looked at the cover and said approximately: *"That's a pretty good-looking resumé you have there, but if Martin says you're good, that's enough for me."*

CHAPTER 14

1979 - 1981

NASA Jet Propulsion Laboratory

S O, IN JUNE of 1979, I started working at JPL. I would continue there for most of the next 15 years. My first project was on an 8-bit microprocessor called the RCA 1802 COSMAC, which was for the Galileo Spacecraft Command Data System. That didn't last long. I wrote some test software for the 1802, but not very much. Meanwhile, Martin was working in a Microcomputer Development Group. They were making a desk-size small business system based on the Z-80 microprocessor with the Digital Research CP/M operating software. They were selling them to other groups at JPL. With Martin's recommendation, I joined that group.

An interesting historical development was that Microsoft MS-DOS was just starting at about that time, 1980. CP/M and MS-DOS were head-to-head competitors, or that's how it seemed to me. Both systems were very rudimentary operating systems for microprocessors, and I wouldn't have said that one was any better than the other. Of course, we know what happened.

I didn't work on the development of that desk computer. I had a series of other small projects. You may not know, but up to that time, computer graphics used a technology called vector graphics. I mentioned being a member of the ACM and the local L.A. chapter. I was also a member of several special interest groups, SIGs. As a member of SIGGRAPH, the Special Interest Group for Computer Graphics, I attended meetings in the 1970s at places like SDC, the Systems Development Corporation in Santa Monica, where I saw demonstrations of the graphics of the time. A vector graphics display is one where the background is the dull green CRT color, and the computer can draw green lines on it. You've probably seen one in some old movie.

Raster graphics was apparently just invented in about 1980. That's the technology that puts colored pixels wherever you want on the screen. We got one of the first color graphics display machines called the CAT-100, and I developed a graphics display package for the Electric Power Plant Simulator. It was difficult and awkward, but I got it to work. It was at that time that I first used an interactive debugger. It was on a Z-80 computer with CP/M.

The Motorola 68000 microprocessor also came out at about that time. We were given what they called a "design module", which was a single board with a 68000 and some supporting chips. This was also not part of a bigger project. I was allowed to just play with it. Imagine that. I learned the Motorola 68000 Assembler Language and I could make the 68000 do some simple things. By coincidence, there was a Data General Eclipse computer in the same room, not being used by anyone. JPL was really a fascinating place, even beyond being part of the Space Program. They had all kinds of machines everywhere. They either bought one of every kind of computer, or were given them, and they never threw any of them away.

So, I took over the Data General computer and programmed it to communicate with the Motorola 68000. To do that, I made an RS-232 cable by hand and connected the two computers together. I implemented a down-line loader and DCU/50 front-end computer resident control program. I think the Motorola 68000 had about the most complex instruction set of any microprocessor and, at that time, it was the most powerful. To assemble my programs, I converted the Motorola 68000 Cross Assembler from IBM 360 Fortran to Data General Eclipse Fortran V.

I developed a complete set of UNIVAC Macros for the 1100/81 to simulate the functions of the JPL Editor for the Voyager Sequence Team.

Then, I was assigned to a really big project called MAFIS, Mobile Automated Field Instrumentation System. This project was funded by the military, and was supposed to be a real-time data collection system for real field exercises. The project was ridiculous. In my estimation, it was probably the biggest failed project JPL ever had. I don't really know that. It's just my guess. They had many people from all over the Lab working on it. They had big meetings to talk about it. One meeting I was in must have had 50 people, but I think I was the only Programmer. My task was to produce some kind of documentation, which, to me, was totally useless. In their meetings, they would talk about traveling around to various stakeholders, gathering requirements. Remember my first job where I learned about negotiating requirements? This experience is my best example of how not doing that leads to a major failure. They never built anything.

MICHAEL DI LORETO

My time in the Microcomputer Development Group was not very long. Those four different projects I just talked about were all done within about a year, maybe less. Then, somehow, I got a job in the JPL Deep Space Network. If that sounds awesome, it's because it was, and still is.

The space ships that have gone to other planets were mostly developed by JPL. You've no doubt heard of the Voyager spacecraft. The Deep Space Network is how JPL communicates with spacecraft that are very far away, in deep space. In order to do that, JPL has three tracking stations positioned in different parts of the world so that there is always a direct line to the outer planets. They are in California, Spain and Australia. As the Earth turns, one of them can always be in touch with the spacecraft. They use huge 70-meter dishes at each site, plus several smaller ones.

I joined a group that made a machine called the Real-Time Combiner (RTC). The reason for it was that, as I heard it, as the spacecraft got farther away, and there were more and more of them, JPL was planning to build a 100-meter dish at some astronomical cost. Instead, some mathematical genius there figured out how to use two antennas, the 70-meter one and another 26-meter one that were already there, to accomplish the same thing.

The idea was that, since the transmitter on the spacecraft had only about the power of a 100-watt lightbulb, and the messages were coming from hundreds of millions of miles away, when the signal arrives at the Earth, it's mostly noise. That is, the signal-to-noise ratio is miniscule. That affects the quality of the pictures we get. The bigger antenna would have improved that. The theory of using two antennas instead was that they would each receive the same signal, but different noise. So, if you added the two signals together, the signal part, being the same, would get stronger, and the noise part, being different would not. Therefore, the signal-to-noise ratio would be improved, and the quality of the pictures we love of Jupiter, Saturn, and so on would be much better.

This idea really worked. Even working on it and knowing what it did, it always seemed like magic to me. The Real-Time Combiner was a single-board computer based on the Intel 8080 microprocessor. It was installed in an electronics rack in the tracking stations, and it received the signals from the two antennas, combined them together to make a better signal, and then passed it on to the next signal processing machine. The real trick was to get the two signals to match. The 70-meter dish was right next to the building at the tracking station that housed all the electronics. The 26-meter dish was a mile or so away. While the signal may have arrived at almost the same time at both antennas, it could go directly from the 70-meter one into the Real-Time Combiner, while the signal from the 26-meter antenna had to be microwaved there, or masered maybe. Even a tiny fraction of a second's difference in the arrival time of the two signals into the Real-Time Combiner was significant. In order to synchronize them, the Real-Time Combiner delayed one of them so the other one could catch up. The way it did that was by other electronics on the same board that were developed by the group I was in before I got there. And because the Earth kept on turning, the amount of delay kept changing, making the process even more tricky.

Madrid DSN Communications Complex

70-Meter Antenna

Goldstone   Madrid   Canberra

Network Operations Control Center at Jet Propulsion Laboratory
Pasadena, California

The Deep Space Communications Complexes

Each complex consists of four Deep Space Stations, equipped with ultra-sensitive receiving systems and large parabolic dish antennas. There are two 34-meter (111-foot) diameter antennas, one 26-meter (85-foot) antenna, and one 70-meter (230-foot) antenna at each complex.

NASA

National Aeronautics and
Space Administration

Jet Propulsion Laboratory
California Institute of Technology
Pasadena, California

I didn't help develop the Real-Time Combiner. It was already done and working when I got there. My part was to maintain them. The software was written in the Intel PL/M programming language on the Intel ISIS microcomputer development system (MDS). I learned the language and used the development system, and I may have fixed a bug or two, but I didn't do that much to the software. A lot of the time, I was receiving defective boards and programming the software into ROM to set up new ones to be sent out to the tracking stations. My title was "Engineer". I even got to visit the tracking station in California one time. It's in the California desert at a place called Goldstone, near Barstow. The managers went to Madrid and Canberra, but I'm not sorry. It was really a very interesting experience, not to mention flying there on JPL's Cessna Citation jet.

The Real-Time Combiner had an Intel 8080 microprocessor along with other Intel parts such as interrupt controller, I/O controller, timer, and so on. Programming it involved using the Intel Data Book, a kind of parts catalog that describes the functioning of each of the chips, and even reading the schematics. I learned a lot about the Intel parts at the most basic level. I was never really an "Engineer". I don't really know electronics. But, always a Programmer, I do understand logic and systems very well.

A problem the Real-Time Combiner had was that it was not really programmed as a real-time system. The software was interrupt-driven, but could not prioritize events. There were failures that I diagnosed as either a lower priority interrupt preempting a higher priority one or vice versa, a higher priority event not preempting a lower priority one. These failures did not happen often enough to compromise the system. It worked fine just about all the time. There was no way to fix it anyway, given the way the software was structured.

My job was to maintain the Real-Time Combiner (RTC) for the NASA JPL Deep Space Network. It was an Intel 8080-based signal processing system with code in real-only memory (EPROM). I used the Intel Microcomputer Development System (MDS) with the ISIS operating system and the PL/M programming language.

I designed and implemented the New RTC Operating System for the second generation Real-Time Combiner, including Multi-Tasking Executive, Command Language, General Purpose Parser, Programmable Lexical Analyzer, General Decision Table Processor and Support Library.

By using the Intel PL/M language, an underlying operating system was not needed because devices could be controlled and interrupts could be handled directly in the PL/M language. To me, that was the right way for a real-time system to work. I did that and a much more elaborate play program for something else. It turned out, though, that none of that was really welcome. The manager even told me they didn't want no multi-tasking. I was gone soon after that, maybe not entirely voluntarily. I was away from JPL for a year and a half, from November 1981 to June 1983.

CHAPTER 15

1981 - 1983

Central Credit, Inc.

J UST THEN, IN November 1981, I got a call out of the blue from Central Credit in Las Vegas. They were upgrading their Data General Eclipse system with RDOS to a new Data General MV/8000 with AOS/VS. They wanted me to come and help out by converting my old Communications Supervisor. I had a contract to do that along with some other work for about a year. The MV/8000 was the subject of the very interesting book *The Soul of a New Machine*.

I lead a team of five consultants to convert their large online system from Data General Eclipse RDOS Fortran IV and Assembler Language to the MV/8000 with AOS/VS and Fortran V. I personally developed the AOS interface packages, the INFOS-II database interface packages and the database recovery logging process. I also converted the Communications Supervisor and Communications Access Manager software which I had developed earlier at Data General.

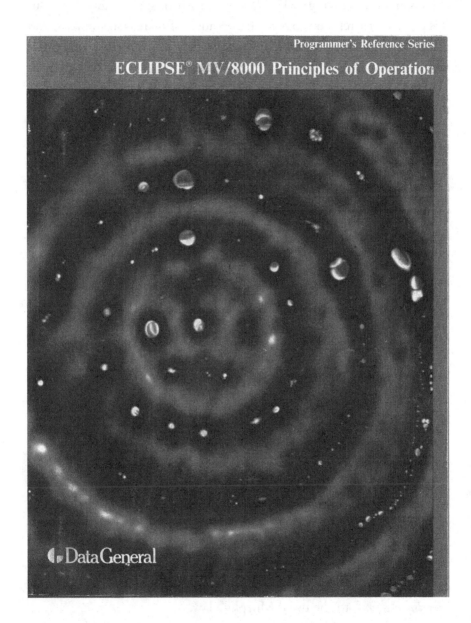

Programmer's Reference Series

ECLIPSE® MV/8000 Principles of Operation

Data General

Murphy's law says approximately, *"If anything can go wrong it will."* I said approximately because the real quotation appears to be different. This is my way of saying it. This law of nature can apply to anything, but it is particularly relevant to software because software is so complex, and at the same time so fragile, that there's pretty much always something that can go wrong. There is an extension to Murphy's law that adds *"at the worst possible time"*. That's good, but for software I would say, *"If anything can go wrong it will, during a demo."*

This sounds pretty discouraging for software development, the idea that things will inevitably go wrong. But I take it as a lesson for programming to preemptively plan for things going wrong by anticipating things that might go wrong and having a strategy for preventing them and recovering from them. Keeping this law in mind is a good programming technique, along with what I constantly tell myself, *"Be more careful."*

When the Central Credit system was more or less complete and most of it was working, the president of the company, Todd Early, tried sending a transaction from a terminal. The program immediately failed. On looking into what happened, I found that there was a space at the end of the line, which confused the parsing code. I've said how parsing can be tricky. I think my mistake was in having a too simple routine that skipped over white space without checking for the end of the line. Of course, in all our testing, which we thought was pretty thorough, this never happened. But the very first thing the customer did blew it up.

When I found out what was wrong, I knew it was my mistake, but I was still kind of indignant. I asked him why he put a space at the end of the line. He said that anyone used to typing on a typewriter always automatically hits the space bar after every word, even the last one. How embarrassing! I'd never heard of that. Logical me, I thought a space was supposed to be used to separate words, not end them. This is why I add *"during a demo"* to the usual Murphy's law.

Years later on the TimeWarp project at JPL, I would use this phenomenon as a software development technique. When we had a new system working and thought we had tested it pretty well, I said,

MICHAEL DI LORETO

"*Let's get the manager to try it.*" I meant to take advantage of the "*during a demo*" extension to Murphy's law. I can't remember now whether the software failed or not when the manager tried it. I just wanted to pass this experience on as a lesson in programming.

CHAPTER 16

January - June 1983

Santa Fe Energy

F ROM ABOUT JANUARY to June of 1983, Merrie Computing Company had a contract with Santa Fe Energy in Santa Fe Springs. The overall project was led by Martin Orton. My part was to do evaluations of a new IBM Instruments 9000 system. It was a desktop workstation based on the Motorola 68000 microprocessor. I wrote programs to test the Operating System, PASCAL compiler and Assembler. I developed a simulator for the Intel 8080 in the Motorola Assembler Language. That program could run CP/M from a floppy disk by intercepting BIOS calls and translating them to IBM Operating System calls.

CHAPTER 17

January - June 1983

California Computer Consultants

ALSO FROM ABOUT January to June of 1983, my old friend, Deborah Runner, had her own company called California Computer Consultants in El Toro. Her husband, Tim Runner, had a project to build an Automotive Emissions Testing System, and Debbie hired me to do the software. It was a real-time system that I wrote in Fortran IV for a Data General MicroNova computer. I worked in a big garage full of exotic imported cars that, I guess, had to be tested for registration in California. The testing system itself was very complex. It had a dynamometer, exhaust gas analyzers, and other things all controlled by the computer. The job was to perform the California standard emissions testing procedures. There were 3 or 4 of them, and they looked like step-by-step procedures. I think one of them was called the California Highway Fuel Economy Test (HFET). I designed the software and implemented it mostly myself, except for several modules that I delegated to Debbie, who did them on her own and then sent them back to me.

My idea then as always was to try to make the program look like the specifications. The prescribed tests were already provided as procedures. That is, they were a series of steps, not like algorithms with loops and branches. My goal was to compose the software as the same series of steps. I did not invent a language for that. Instead, I wrote every distinct function as a Fortran subroutine, and then wrote sequential procedures as a series of subroutine calls. When this was done, I printed the procedures and presented them to Debbie and Tim. Tim was the overall manager of the project. He was not a Programmer himself, but he was very computer savvy. Of course, Debbie was an expert Programmer. When Tim looked at my Fortran procedures, he could see that they matched the California published procedures and he was amazed. He said he'd never seen anything like that. As a non-programmer, he could read the code. Not only that, but even better, he could verify that the code was correct.

I like talking about my theory of programming. I've mentioned how I think that most applications can be divided into two parts, one part is composed of the application-specific functionality, and the other part is infrastructure that makes the program work. The infrastructure part is about what you would expect, data structures and algorithms. The application part is what the customer is interested in. It's what he expects the program to do to get the results he wants. I've called the disconnect between the customer, the programmer and the computer a communication problem. By that I mean there is distortion in the information that goes from the customer to the programmer, and then more distortion when the program is coded. The trouble is that the customer doesn't know what the program is really going to do until it's done and he can see the results. No amount of documentation can solve this problem, contrary to what most managers think. The only true documentation is the program code itself. That code is not normally readable by the customer, even for someone who is highly technical. Often, it's not even readable by Programmers.

Admittedly, the division of a program into application code and what I call "system" code takes some creativity on the part of the program designer. Defining the application as a set of distinct functions may require even more thought. It's hard to explain how to go about doing that, but I've found that, when you try, it gets to be straightforward. Now, you know a computer program is a set of instructions in some order. When the set of functions is defined for an application, it becomes, in effect, the application's instruction set, as I see it. Once you have a complete set of application-specific instructions, you put them in order to program the application. I sometimes call that a programming language for a specific application, but it doesn't have to involve designing a new language. In the example just given, it was a just a set of Fortran subroutine calls.

I've read some theory of programming that said that subroutines should be some particular size, not too big and not too small. Supposedly, code that is about a page of code or less is more easily digestible by a Programmer. My idea is that a subroutine should do just one thing, no matter how much code it takes. By doing just one thing, the subroutine becomes an instruction in the application-specific instruction set. That might be more than one page of code, and that's okay. If a subroutine gets too big, though, it should probably be broken down into smaller pieces. That doesn't change the application's instruction set, it's just a matter of organization. Now, it can be somewhat disconcerting when a function is one line of code. Programmers kind of naturally resist the idea that a subroutine can have just one line of code inside, with all the wrapping of a subroutine and having to think of a name for it, and so on. Instead of calling a subroutine, why not just write that one line of code?

My answer is that, when an application has clearly defined functions, it is much more understandable, much more maintainable, and much more reliable. I would also argue that, even with the big detour involved in the design of such an application, it does not take longer to finish the job. A little more time up front means a lot less time at the end, debugging and changing code. Obvious, right? I can just hear someone saying: *"Oh, I thought that was really something, but now that you explained it, I can see it was nothing at all."*

I've talked about RPG, but I never said what it was. It stands for Report Program Generator. I've also called it a programming language, and it works like one because you write programs using it, but it's really not. RPG generates programs from specifications. There were 4 different specification forms: file description, input, calculations and output. Each form had fixed fields to be filled in. The file description form described a file on one line. The input form described the layout of input records. The output form described the layout of the output records, which could be to a file or to a printed report. The calculation form allowed a series of steps for simple calculations with some conditionality based on indicators.

These specification forms described the application functionality in a mostly declarative way, except for the calculation steps. All the machinery to make the program work was built in, including even matching input files by key for updating a master file with transactions. Very substantial business application programs were created this way. I think my ideas for building systems like this came from RPG. I don't really have any original ideas, just borrowed ones.

CHAPTER 18

June - August 1983

JPL - Instrument Development Group

W HEN THAT WAS done, I went back to JPL, recommended again by Martin Orton. It was now mid-1983. I joined The Instrument Development Group where I did two new projects by myself. First, I developed the software for a Real-Time Telemetry Decommutation system for the Airborne Imaging Spectrometer (AIS). It was in the Assembler Language on a DEC PDP 11/40 with RT11. The computer was very old. It had core memory, and not much of it, maybe 16k bytes? RT11 was their real-time executive, very small, and actually good. The computer and other equipment were in a small room that was just big enough for the machines and a chair. JPL was really interesting like that, old buildings with all kinds of machines in little rooms and even in corridors.

The telemetry from the AIS was on a magnetic tape, but it was not a tape like you're used to seeing. Magnetic tape drives on computers start and stop when a block of data, or a record, is read. The tape is going very fast, so it looks like it's spinning continuously, but it's not. The tape drive for reading the telemetry tape was bigger, I think it was taller than me, and it read the tape continuously like a tape recorder. I think it might even have been analog data on the tape that was digitized by the tape drive controller.

The computer did not control the tape drive. You pushed a button on the tape drive and it started reading and didn't stop. That's what made this a genuine real-time problem. The software had to capture the data as it was flying by and record it onto a disk. Too bad I don't remember the details now, but a typical real-time program the way I used to do it was to have separate tasks for reading and writing. The reading task would have higher priority so that, as soon as the data was ready, it would grab the data and put it in a queue for the writing task. The writing task would take the data from the queue and write it on the disk, more or less at its leisure. It couldn't take too much time, though, because of the limited amount of memory for the queue of data. Both tasks were time-critical. When I talk about real-time programs, they're mostly like that.

Another thing about the PDP 11/40 was that it did not have multiply and divide instructions. I needed that, so I "invented" my own multiply and divide algorithms. This was not the only time I did that. The Data General NOVA also did not have multiply and divide instructions and I had to "invent" them again.

One time, I was at a Computer Architecture conference in Hawaii, and there was someone there giving a talk about the new RISC (Reduced Instruction Set Computer) technology. He was making the point that it was better to have fewer, faster instructions, and that more complex instructions could be handled by software. There was something to that. By having fewer and simpler instructions, instructions that could execute in one cycle, the processor could be smaller and cheaper, and it was argued that the system would go faster overall because the simpler instructions were much more frequent than the more complex ones. The point he was making was something like, *"Imagine a computer that does not have multiply and divide hardware. They could be implemented in software."* What he apparently thought was a great revelation struck me as just funny. I had already had so much fun writing multiply and divide software for old computers that didn't have those instructions.

After that I developed the real-time Ground Support Equipment (GSE) software for the JPL Internal Discharge Monitor (IDM), an instrument on the CRRES satellite. That was in the 8086 Assembler Language on an IBM PC with MS-DOS. Ground Support Equipment at JPL was a test system for what they called an "instrument". An instrument was a computer system on a satellite or spacecraft that gathered data from some specialized device. There were usually several of these instruments on a satellite or spacecraft doing different things. They were all coordinated by a Command Data System (CDS), which was another computer system on the spacecraft.

MS-DOS, of course, was not real-time at all. It didn't have multitasking and I don't think you could even handle interrupts. The GSE was a real-time system, though, because telemetry data and images were arriving at their own speed and the software had to keep up with them. An interesting challenge for me was that I had to make a graphic display on the PC screen, and with no graphics software, I had to put the images directly into the screen buffer memory.

CHAPTER 19

1983 - 1985

JPL - Joint Theater Level
Simulation (JTLS)

T HEN I WENT to a different group where I worked on the
Joint Theater Level Simulation (JTLS) for 2 years. This was
a very big project funded by the U.S. Military. It was an interactive
war game system on a VAX 11/780. There were three major parts to
the system. The simulation itself, called the Combat Events Program,
was developed by a small company in Monterey whose people were
associated with the Naval Post-Graduate School there. The system had
nine terminals for the players: 4 for each side and 1 controller. The user
interface to the simulation was called the Model Interface Program.
That was done at JPL by a small group led by Martin Orton. The third
part was the Database Preparation Program. That was my part. Where
the other two parts had groups of 4 or 5 people, my part was just me.

The Combat Events Program was written in the Simscript II
programming language. The reason for using that language was that it
was good for Discrete Event Simulation. One of its features was that it
could read data from a file by saying "read" and the name of a variable.
It didn't matter how big the data was or its type. It was free-form
separated by white space. That same "read" statement could read more
than one variable, and besides being simple variables, they could be
arrays and complex data structures. The "read" statement did dynamic
memory allocation to make space for the variables. The Combat Events
Program was "data driven". That is, everything that could possibly be

made into input data was included in a big file the program read when it started up. That big text file was what the Database Preparation Program was supposed to create.

The VAX had an SQL relational database management system called INGRES. Naturally, since the Database Preparation Program had "database" in its name, the managers thought it needed a database management system. I had two ideas about that. One was that a text file with variables, arrays and data structures did not seem to me to fit well with tables of rows and columns. The other was that INGRES was a big system that used a lot of resources. You may not know this. The VAX 11/780, called the "Computer of the 80s" by DEC, was kind of a super-minicomputer. It was considered to be a very powerful timesharing system. The way computer power used to be measured was in millions of instructions per second, or MIPS. The computer manufacturers worked out some way to compensate for the differences in instruction sets so that they could all be measured in MIPS and compared to each other. The standard was the VAX 11/780 with 1 MIP.

I think the tool should fit the task at hand. But often Programmers are given some software package they're supposed to use for their job, and then spend most of their time fighting with the tool to get it to do what they want. I knew that. So, I rejected the relational database approach and wrote the program myself. Now, there was a rule on the project handed down from the Military sponsors that all software would be written in Simscript. I'm always happy to learn a new language, so I started writing my program like that. I got to know the language pretty well, but it was giving me a lot of trouble. It was not really suited to what I was trying to do. It was good at simulation, but not at the kind of data manipulation I needed. One day I said something like that to a guy who was the system manager of the VAX, and he said: "*Why don't you use C?*" I said: "*What's that?*" He told me, and I thought it was interesting, so I gave it a try.

In 1983 the C language was new. I hadn't heard of it before. I liked it because it was very low-level. Not as low as Assembler Language, but closer to the machine than other high-level languages. I could make any data structure I wanted and have total control over it. I was soon doing my whole program in C and it was much better. But that was against the rules. When the sponsors found out about it they called a meeting at JPL. They would say they wanted everything to be in Simscript because when we at JPL finished the job we would turn the software over to their Programmers, and they only knew Simscript. I would say they could learn C and would be glad to do so. Fortunately for me, there was an Army Colonel at JPL overseeing the project, and he agreed with me. So I won the debate, and my program was written in C.

It then turned out that, since I wasn't using a database management system, they stopped saying the data was in a database, and began using the term 'scenario' instead. My program changed from being the Database Preparation Program to the Scenario Preparation Program.

My approach to this problem was similar to what I described as how I did the Assemblers for the microprogrammable controllers. That is, the so-called "scenario" didn't have any real specifications. The Combat Events Program was underway and had a text file with all its data. I had a copy of the program that I used to find out what data was in the file, in what order, and what types and structures it was in. I assumed the file could change as they further developed the program. Therefore, I invented a specification language to describe the data in the text file. Then I embedded that language into a tool that had been developed at JPL called the System Design and Documentation Language (SDDL). The purpose of that tool was to produce formal documentation. It formatted the pages, generated an index, and so on. It made the document look nice. To me, readability of the software was very important, so that all worked out very well.

My Scenario Preparation Program was to have a user interface where someone could view the data, make changes to it, add new things, and save a new file. I did that by designing screen formats for all the various data, with menus for navigation, about 100 screens in all. For that, I invented another specification language to layout the screen formats. Again, I embedded the specifications in SDDL to make it look more professional.

I used to say: *"The Scenario Preparation Program works by reading the documentation."*

I said I did the whole project by myself, but I did have an assistant for a short time. He was a student at Caltech who had a Summer internship at JPL and was assigned to me. I don't think his major was Computer Science. It seems like it was Mathematics or Physics. Whatever, he was a really smart guy. I gave him the task of testing the Scenario Preparation Program. As I said, there were about 100 different screens and they all needed to be checked out. I showed him how to run the program once, but I didn't have to tell him what to do. He didn't ask any questions, he just figured everything out himself. He was terrific. He would methodically go through every screen and try everything. I didn't watch him. I would just come in in the morning and he would give me a list of the things he found wrong the day before. He was very thorough. He not only tried everything the program was supposed to do, he deliberately did things that were wrong, like hitting random keys on the keyboard. The defects he found were not major bugs in the software. But, as you would expect with such a large user interface, there were mistakes. I was not embarrassed by that. I would take his list and spend the day making corrections. I was so grateful. I can't tell you how much it benefitted my program to have someone like that testing it.

Naturally, I would highly recommend having a brilliant person like that to do your testing for you. It's a lesson for any software project. However, good luck finding him. I've had assistants on other projects where I spent more time helping them than they saved time for me.

The VAX computer we were using belonged to the JPL Graphics Lab, made famous by Jim Blinn who did the graphics for *The Mechanical Universe* there. I saw him working on it. We had VT-100 terminals lined up on tables in a work room. One day I was in the work room and the manager of the Graphics Lab came to me to say there was something wrong. My program was causing a highly excessive number of page faults. I hadn't noticed it, but he did because he was monitoring the system's statistics. I looked and it was true. And it was bad because it was affecting the system's performance overall, a system we were sharing with Jim Blinn.

VAX VMS page faults forward. That is, when there is a page fault, it automatically causes more page faults in the direction of higher memory addresses. The reason for that is that programs execute from lower to higher addresses, and, generally, data is accessed from lower to higher addresses too, especially for structures like arrays. By anticipating future page faults, the system gets better virtual memory performance. What I discovered, though, was that the memory allocator in the VAX C library, *malloc*, allocated memory from higher addresses down. I think they got this algorithm from a book because it seemed to me I had seen it before. It was an example of clever programming. The trouble, of course, was that, by accessing memory from higher memory addresses to lower, it was thwarting the VMS algorithm and causing worse performance.

How to fix that? I wrote a new memory allocator of my own. And how did I know how to do that? I'd done it before. As soon as I did that, the excessive page fault problem was solved. I don't count that as a bug on my part, but I did have bugs in my program. I always solved them right away, though, so they never slowed me down. I remember someone there telling me he thought I was a very fast Programmer and thinking to myself that I probably didn't write code any faster than anyone else. It was just that I spent a lot less time debugging, both from fixing bugs faster and from not creating as many bugs in the first place.

A large part of the database, which was actually in a separate text file, was the terrain database. The terrain in the combat simulation was represented by hexagons, or hexes, where each hex had a numeric value that indicated the type of terrain (desert, mountain, ocean, etc.) and each of the six sides had a numeric value that indicated the type of barrier (road, bridge, impassible, etc.). There was an eighth value that I don't remember now. So there were eight numbers for each hex, and there were many thousands of them. The terrain database was created from either an aerial or a satellite image of a real place in the world. It was the JPL Image Processing Lab that turned the image into hexes. I got the terrain database from them.

At first, I tried to print it. It made a big pile of paper that was pretty much unintelligible. So that was no good. The famous Graphics Lab had several graphics machines. I found an old AED512 color graphics terminal in a corner of the machine room, and "borrowed" it for myself. It had a serial interface where you could send it commands to draw lines, fill boxes, change colors, and so on. I wrote a program to read the terrain data file and draw hexes. I colored the hexes and the sides according to a simple scheme like green for mountain, brown for desert, etc.

One day I was sitting in the terminal room by myself, I had just started working on my program, and the Section Manager walked by and asked me what I was doing. I told him and he said he was just leaving on a trip for a few days, and he would be very impressed if he could see it when he came back. Naturally, it was working when he got back, and he was impressed. The color display actually looked like a real map of the area. It was really great!

As a consequence of that, it was easy to see defects in the data. An impassible barrier at the edge of the map was missing. A road was disconnected. Things you would never be able to find poring over the data but were obvious when you could see a complete picture. I then made a way to interactively fix things directly on the screen. Data visualization is really valuable.

We often went to Monterey to visit the computer room at the Naval Post-Graduate School. They happened to have RAMTEK 9460 color graphics machines in the computer room, so I adapted my program to display the terrain data on them. It was a cool thing. Everybody liked it.

I also made my Terrain Database Hex Editor program work on the Gould/Deanza graphics display system in the JPL Image Processing Lab where the terrain data came from. I also traveled to the US Army Concepts Analysis Agency (CAA) in Washington, D.C. (really Maryland), to port my program to their Tektronix 4015 graphics display terminal. Years later, long after leaving JPL, I would have a small contract to travel to Jackson, Mississippi to make my program work for the US Army Corps of Engineers on a graphics display machine they had there.

ARCHITECTURE HANDBOOK

When the project was close to being done, approaching the deadline according to the contract between JPL and the Military, the system didn't work. It had serious problems and, if it didn't make the deadline, the project risked being canceled. JPL had a thing they called a "Tiger Team", which was when they assembled experts from around the Lab when a project was in trouble. In this case, the "Tiger Team" was me.

MICHAEL DI LORETO

The problems were in the Combat Events Program. I went to Monterey and worked for several days by myself in an empty classroom. It was very cold and there were no students, so it must have been during a Winter break. It was so cold water dripped on me from the ceiling. I tried wearing gloves, but then I couldn't type. My manager, Mike DeGyurky, was there too, and he visited me from time to time to encourage me and to see how it was going.

The Programmers who wrote the Combat Events Program were good. They knew what they were doing as far as the simulation was concerned. But they didn't quite get VMS System Services. Most of that had to do with communicating with the Model Interface Program. There were a lot of different problems and, as is my way, I went through them one by one until they were all solved. I was all alone working in that cold room for several days, and I didn't think at all about what everyone else on the project was doing. I guess they were all waiting for me.

In the end, the project was a success, and continued on for several years. I was named "Systems Engineer", a kind of management title that's usually reserved for employees. I was neither a manager nor an employee, but I was in charge of the whole project. As the leader now, I put VT-100 terminals in the Programmers' offices. That was shocking in the mid-1980s. Programmers with their own terminals on their desks! Unheard of. Lazy programmers.

My last task was to put the software onto a magnetic tape and deliver it to the Pentagon. Yeah. Really. The real Pentagon. I went to Washington, D.C. (actually Virginia) and walked up to the front door of the Pentagon, showed them my papers, and they let me in! Someone led me down a wide walkway that seemed to be going underground and then showed me a very small room, more like a closet, where they had a VAX and a chair. I went in there, mounted the tape, and copied the software onto their disk. Maybe I checked to make sure it would start. But that was it. The project was done and delivered.

During the JTLS project, I traveled many times to the Naval Post-Graduate School in Monterey, CA., once to the Army War College in Carlyle, PA., and once to the Concepts Analysis Agency (CAA) in Washington D.C. Those were our three customer sites. I also traveled once to the United States Readiness Command (REDCOM) headquarters in Tampa, FL. They were the sponsor of our project. And I went to the US Warrior Preparation Center in Germany two times.

Later, JPL got a follow-on contract to develop the Joint Exercise Support System (JESS). Martin Orton worked on the Model Interface part of it again, but I didn't do anything. That project took my Scenario Preparation Program (SPP) and used my two specification languages to describe the data and screens for the new system. Maybe someone asked me a question once. To me, this further validated my approach. By having general specifications that are both human and computer readable, systems can be developed faster, changed easier, are more reliable, and can sometimes even be reused for another project. The JESS project was also able to use the C language since, after what I had gone through, it was okay now.

Years later, I had a one-day contract from Roland & Associates, the company who developed the Combat Events Program for JTLS and who was continuing to maintain it, to go to Monterey to make JTLS work on the DEC Alpha workstation, a 64-bit RISC machine. There was some small difference between the Alpha and the VAX that was causing the program to not start. I don't remember what that difference was now, but I fixed it pretty much right away. Jay Roland flew me there and back from San Jose in his private plane.

CHAPTER 20

1985 - 1989

JPL - Time Warp Operating System

AFTER JTLS, I stayed on at JPL in the same building, but on a new project: *Timewarp on the Hypercube*. Really. That's what it was called. *Timewarp* was the name of an operating system for Distributed Discrete Event Simulation, and the *Hypercube* was a large-scale distributed multiprocessor. The Time Warp Operating System (TWOS) was invented by Dave Jefferson, a Computer Science professor at UCLA. The Hypercube Parallel Processing system was built by Caltech. The project was funded by the U.S. Military to potentially do more war games.

Applications running under the Time Warp Operating System were Object-Oriented and coded in C. The operating model was similar to Smalltalk in that it worked by objects sending messages to each other or to themselves. It was not so much a programming language like C++, which wouldn't be available for a few more years. The way this worked for Discrete Event Simulations was that the messages were stamped with the simulation time. In the Simscript language I described earlier, the equivalent notion was called scheduling an event. TWOS ordered the messages by simulation time and then executed the destination object's code for each message, advancing the simulation time for each one.

When I joined the project, there were 4 or 5 people already working on it. It was not in very good shape, though. Each person had his own version of TimeWarp, and none of them worked. The computer we had to use was that same VAX 11/780 in the JPL Graphics Lab. Software organization is one of my strengths. That's not normally mentioned as an attribute of programming, but I think it's important. I kind of took over and made one good version of the software and got rid of all the rest. Then everyone used the version I controlled. I was not the boss or the technical leader of the project. Nobody had to obey me. It's just that I was doing something useful.

An interesting thing we did as a project was to have regular configuration control board meetings. These were run by the manager and everyone was included. Normally I would not like something like that but, in this case, it was simple and effective. The idea is that the "configuration" of the software is basically what's in it, what features does it have, and so forth, and that there should be some control over it. That is, there should be some control over what new features are added to the software, when and how. In the meetings, anyone could make a suggestion for a new feature or some change to the software. Then everyone in the meeting could discuss it. It just kind of worked out, since I was personally in charge of the software, that I was the best one to evaluate the proposals. I could judge not so much whether the change was a good idea or not, but what kind of effect it would have on the system and how difficult it would be to do. I'm naturally receptive to new ideas, so there was never really any dispute, although I'm also naturally pretty strict about the integrity of the software. Usually I'd be the one to implement the changes anyway, so I was always able to make sure they were okay.

 The Jet Propulsion Laboratory

Presents the

Technology and Applications Programs Group Achievement Award

for the

Time Warp Operating Systems Development Team

to

Michael A. Diloreto

In recognition of pioneering achievements in applying large scale microprocessor supercomputers to irregular problems, specifically parallel discrete-event simulation.

Signed at Pasadena, California,
this twenty-second day of October,
nineteen hundred and ninety-three

Malvin L. Yeater, Assistant Laboratory Director
Office of Technology & Applications Programs

Edward C. Stone, Director
Jet Propulsion Laboratory

We were doing pretty well with TimeWarp running on the VAX. Then we got a real Hypercube. It was made of 32 Intel 8086 processors. The way they're connected together is the hypercube topology. It's like a cube, but with more dimensions. Processing nodes are not connected directly to every other node. To get a message from a node at one corner of the hypercube to another one at another corner, it would have to be routed through some other nodes. It's basically a simple idea, but actually making it work can be pretty complicated.

There was a separate part of the software called the Machine Interface that was supposed to deal directly with the 8086 microprocessors. That was not used on the VAX, so even though the TimeWarp part of the operating system was kind of okay, the 8086 part was not. The project had been going on for at least a couple of years before I got there. In the Summers, a professor of Computer Science and Mathematics at Florida State University came to JPL to work on the project. His name was Steve Bellenot. He came for the Summer again when I was there, and we worked together on making TimeWarp work on the Hypercube.

National Aeronautics and
Space Administration

Presents This Certificate to

MICHAEL A. DiLORETO

Certificate of Recognition

For the creative development of a technical innovation which has been proposed for publication as a NASA Tech Brief entitled ...

TIME WARP OPERATING SYSTEM VERSION 2.0 (TWOS)

Carroll C. Dicim March 13, 1991

Chairman, Inventions and Contributions Board   Date

By now, the contract deadline for the project was that Fall. If TimeWarp was not working on the Hypercube by then, the project would be canceled. Steve and I worked on it every day for 2 or 3 months that Summer, 1986 I think. Steve had been on the project longer, and he understood the theory of TimeWarp better than me. I happened to be an expert in Intel processors and parts, and really good at debugging. We were a good team. We complemented each other's strengths.

I'm pretty innovative too. I found several VT-100 terminals, maybe 4 or 5 of them, and connected them to some of the Hypercube nodes. That way, the software could print things and we could even get into the debugger. Sometimes software is so bad that it would have been faster to rewrite it than to debug it. The trouble is you don't know that until you've been debugging for awhile, and then you think you're almost there. The Machine Interface code was like that. It took the two of us a couple of months to get it to work. But we did it. It worked, there was a demo, and the project was renewed for another year. It would actually go on for several years more.

OSBORNE/McGraw-Hill

THE
8086
BOOK
includes the 8088

Russell Rector - George Alexy

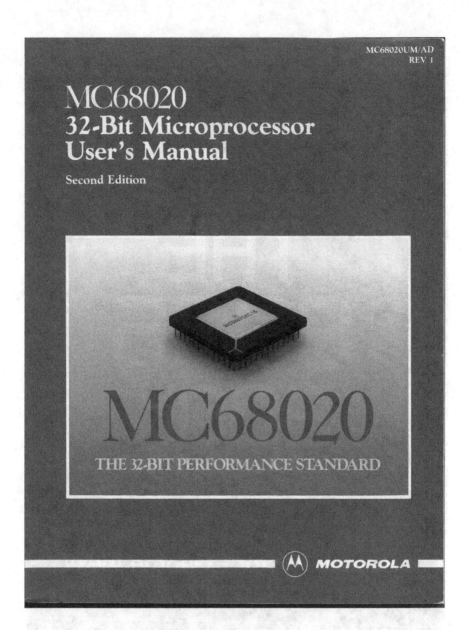

MC68020
**32-Bit Microprocessor
User's Manual**

Second Edition

MC68020

THE 32-BIT PERFORMANCE STANDARD

Ⓜ *MOTOROLA*

Caltech built a Mark III Hypercube that was 256 Motorola 68020 processors, two per each node. Brian Beckman was the real technical lead of the project. He had a PhD in Astrophysics from Princeton, and he was a bonafide genius, to me he was anyway. We were in the so-called Foothill offices of JPL in Pasadena, and the Mark III Hypercube was installed at the main Lab. He suggested we could make TimeWarp work on that much

MICHAEL DI LORETO

bigger and better Hypercube, and he knew the people to give us access to it. So, we went there on a weekend, and working together we made it work. I happened to know the Motorola 68000 already. On Monday, we announced the good news, and the manager was mad. He didn't like being left out. But we didn't get fired because it really was a giant step forward for our project. Now we could access the Mark III Hypercube remotely, and we never used the Mark II Hypercube, the 8086 one, again.

Our group was maybe the first one at JPL to get Sun Workstations. Each one of us had our own Sun 3 Workstation on our desk. To me, that was as big an advance in technology as timesharing had been over punched cards, maybe bigger. I made a version of TimeWarp that used our local network of Suns, which included a Sun 4 SPARC, as a multiprocessor system.

The Time Warp Operating System was written entirely in C, except for a little bit of Assembler Language code for each type of machine for context switching. That included the Sun SPARC, which was an advanced RISC machine. The machine actually had a lot of instructions, so I didn't think the instruction set was particularly reduced. I guess what qualified it as RISC was that the instructions were all one word and executed in one cycle. The Motorola 68020 was a CISC machine (Complex Instruction Set Computer). The instructions were variable length and executed in multiple cycles on variable length data. The IBM 360 was a CISC machine for the same reasons, although other computers like the UNIVAC 1108 worked according to the way I just described as RISC, since it had single word instructions that executed in one cycle, but didn't get that title.

The Sun SPARC architecture was designed with the C language in mind. C has a run-time stack for passing arguments to subroutines and for holding local variables. In general, CPUs are faster than memories, so instructions that operate on registers inside the CPU are faster than instructions that access memory. That's normal for most computers. The SPARC went one step further by having a very large number of registers and then mapping a local stack frame to a group of them. So, references to the stack could access registers instead of memory and go faster. When another subroutine is called, the new stack frame is mapped to another set of registers. They referred to that as a sliding window. This was effective because C programs generally have a lot of calls and returns with stack frames that are usually pretty small. Of course, there is memory behind the register stack and that's used when the registers run out. To switch context to another task, or in the case of TWOS, to another object, the registers all have to be saved, and you needed Assembler Language code to do that.

The Sun Workstation could do graphics on its big screen. I made a way for TimeWarp on the Mark III Hypercube to make a log of all the events on each node in its local memory and, at the end of a simulation, dump all the logs out into a file. Discrete Event Simulation works by scheduling events in the future. The simulation engine advances the simulation to the time of the next scheduled event and then runs the code for the event. That in turn can schedule more events, and so it goes. The idea of a TimeWarp distributed simulation is that each processing node can move ahead in simulation time independently of the other nodes. But then a node can receive a message for an event that's in the past relative to that node's current simulation time. When that happens, the future messages have to be canceled and the simulation rolled back. That's accomplished by sending anti-messages. When messages and anti-messages collide they're annihilated. This strategy was called optimistic because the future messages can be right.

My log entries contained both real time and simulation time, the sending and receiving nodes, and the type of message, either positive or negative. I wrote a program to do a two-dimensional display of that information, using the two times for x and y coordinates, and the two nodes for the ends of lines. When I ran that, it made a graphic of the whole simulation on one screen. You could see messages going forward and backward.

At that time, the Sun screen was monochrome. But I found a Silicon Graphics IRIS color graphics workstation in a room by itself with nobody using it. Again, JPL was so cool! There was a little room with an IRIS workstation and a chair just across the hall from my office. I took it over and made my program work on it, using colors for the lines, green for positive messages and red for negative messages.

That made the graphic simulation results much better. Dave Jefferson presented papers at simulation conferences and used images that I produced in his presentations. I didn't get to go. But I think this is why when one day there were some VIP visitors, and the manager was showing them around, introducing everybody, and when he came to me he said: *"That's Mike. We just let him do whatever he wants and we always get something good."*

I created the TimeWarp Message Graph, the TimeWarp Execution Graph and the TimeWarp Object Activity Display, first on the Sun, and then on the IRIS workstation.

Steve Bellenot came back for another Summer. This time he had an idea for a different way to display my simulation log data. He proposed a circle with positions around the circle that represented the nodes of the 7-dimensional Hypercube. Messages from one node to another would go from one place on the circle to another one. That takes trigonometry, which he not I could easily do. We always preferred the IRIS workstation now because of its color display, so we used that. We modified my graphics program to draw a circle and plot the messages in color there. Instead of a static graph, it made an animated 2D display of the TimeWarp message activity that was almost like a video. It looked like a brain working. Everyone wanted to see it.

We called it the *HyperCircle*. It was very impressive to see, but it also did something practical. As it was running, there appeared a small gap in time where no messages were sent or received, and it was very visible. The underlying software was developed by a group at the main Lab. We reported this phenomenon to them and, knowing what to look for, they were able to reproduce it, and thus able to fix it. We found a real problem with a play program.

Steve wrote a paper about this and presented it at the 1989 Eastern Multiconference of the Society for Computer Simulation. He called it *Tools For Measuring The Performance and Diagnosing The Behavior Of Distributed Simulations Using Time Warp*. He made me his co-author from the California Institute of Technology. It wasn't wrong. The HyperCube was a joint project between JPL and Caltech, and besides that, Caltech was the administrator of JPL and my paychecks came from Caltech. There were several other papers where I was credited as one of the co-authors from JPL. They were all written by others in our team. I only did software.

NEWSLETTER of

THE SOCIETY FOR COMPUTER SIMULATION

Winter 1989

Highlighted Inside:
**1989 Eastern
Multiconference
Preliminary Program**
March 28-31, 1989
Tampa, Florida

★ **Simulators VI**
Featuring Nuclear Power Plant Training

★ **Artificial Intelligence & Simulation**
With a series of Tutorials

★ **MAPCON V**
High Performance Digital Computers for Scientific
Computations

★ Distributed Simulation
★ Tools for the Simulationist
★ The Twenty-Second Annual Simulation
Symposium

...And, Many More Interesting Features

MICHAEL DI LORETO

CONFERENCE: DISTRIBUTED SIMULATION

CHAIR: Brian Unger, *University of Calgary*
PROGRAM CHAIR: Richard Fujimoto, *University of Utah*

PLENARY TALK: PARALLEL SIMULATION AS A FUNDAMENTAL ISSUE IN COMPUTER SCIENCE
David Jefferson, *UCLA*

Until recently discrete event simulation has seemed more of a tool or application domain than a central computational paradigm. But research into parallel simulation reveals exciting fundamental issues that force us to think differently about both parallel computation in general and simulation in particular. In this talk we describe some bizarre and apparently paradoxical phenomena that arise from the study of parallel simulation.

1) To achieve speedup from parallelism it is often necessary to execute simulation events out of order, and then undo and redo some events later to fix the results.

2) The total amount of work done in a parallel simulation may be many times greater than when the same simulation is executed sequentially, yet it can still run many times faster.

3) Parallel simulation provides fundamental insight into basic computer science issues such as fault tolerance and dynamic load management.

4) Considerations arising from parallel simulation and the Time Warp mechanism suggest the possibility of a dualism between "computation" and "anticomputation" that has no counterpart in other computational paradigms, and offers possibilities for new kinds of speedup not yet throughly understood.

OPTIMISTIC PERFORMANCE EVALUATION

Performance measurements of the JPL implementation of the Time Warp simulation mechanism are presented. The authors report significant speedups across a variety of discrete event simulation applications.

Performance of the colliding pucks simulation on the time warp operating systems (Part 1: Asynchronous behavior and sectoring)
Philip Hontalas, Brian Beckman, Mike Di Loreto, Leo Blume, Peter Reiher, Kathy Sturdevant, L. Van Warren, John Wedel and Fred Wieland, *Jet Propulsion Laboratory*, David Jefferson, *UCLA.*

Benchmarking the time warp operating system with a computer network simulation
Matthew Presley, *Harvey Mudd College*, Frederick Weiland, *Jet Propulsion Laboratories*, Maria Ebling, *Carnegie-Mellon University*, David Jefferson, *UCLA*

Distributed combat simulation and time warp: The model and its performance
Frederick Wieland, Lawrence Hawley, Abe Feinberg, Mike Di Loreto, Leo Blume, Joseph Ruffles, Brian Beckman, Philip Hontalas and Steve Bellenot, *Jet Propulsion Laboratory*, David Jefferson, *UCLA*

An ant foraging model implemented on the time warp operating system
Maria Ebling, *Carnegie-Mellon University*, David Jefferson, *UCLA*, Matthew Presley, *Harvey Mudd College*, Michael Di Loreto and Frederick Wieland, *Jet Propulsion Laboratory*

CONSERVATIVE PERFORMANCE EVALUATION

Performance evaluations of the Chandy-Misra-Bryant simulation mechanisms, and new variations of that approach, are presented.

Techniques for efficient shared-memory parallel simulation
David B. Wagner, Edward D. Lazowska and Brian N. Bershad, *University of Washington*

Variants of the Chandy-Misra-Bryant distributed discrete-event simulation algorithm
Wen-King Su and Charles L. Seitz, *California Institute of Technology*

The effects of feedback on the performance of conservative algorithms
Edwina Leung, *Jade Simulations International Corporation*, John Cleary, *University of Calgary*, Greg Lomow, Dirk Baeznel, Brian Unger, *Jade Simulations International Corporation*

COMPUTATION MODELS

Papers in this session define new underlying frameworks and computation models for concurrent simulation.

Space-Time and simulation
K. Mani Chandy, *California Inst. of Tech.*, Rivi Sherman, *ISI-University of Southern Calif.*

Balanced sequencing protocols
Yeturu Aahlad and J. C. Browne, *University of Texas at Austin*

Mapping hierarchical discrete event models to multiprocessor systems: concepts, algorithm and simulation
Guoqing Zhang, *ZYCAD*, Bernard P. Zeigler, *University of Arizona*

OPTIMISTIC METHODS

New techniques and modeling tools related to Time Warp are presented.

Algorithmic optimizations of simulations on time warp
Dirk Baezner, *Jade Simulations Int'l. Corporation*, John Cleary, *University of Calgary*, Greg Lomow and Brian W. Unger, *Jade Simulations International Corporation*

18

Object creation, messaging, and state manipulation in an object oriented time warp system
Peter A. Tinker and Jonathan R. Agre, *Rockwell International Corporation*

Simulation of time warp distributed simulations
Jonathan R. Agre, *Rockwell International Corporation*

CONSERVATIVE METHODS

Novel conservative simulation algorithms and performance evaluations are presented.

The conditional event approach to distributed simulation
K. M. Chandy, *California Institute of Technology,* R. Sherman, *USC/Information Sci Institute*

Scalability of the bounded lag distributed discrete event simulation
Boris D. Lubachevsky, *Bell Laboratories*

The distributed simulation of clustered processes
Bojan Groselj and Carl Tropper, *McGill University*

A parallel simulation scheme based on distances between objects
Rassul Ayani, *The Royal Institute of Technology*

WORK IN PROGRESS

Mini presentations of 5-10 minutes each of current work in progress in concurrent simulation. Solicitations of presentations will take place both before and during the conference.

CONTINUOUS AND TIME STEPPED METHODS

Important issues and performance evaluation studies related to time-driven and continuous simulations are presented.

Dynamic remapping of parallel time-stepped simulations
David M. Nicol, *College of William and Mary*

Modeling and discrete event simulation using concurrent programming in a CACSD package.
Andre Geiser, Daniel Burkhalter and Magnus Rimvall, *Swiss Federal Institute of Technology*

Automated parallelization of serial simulations for hypercube parallel processors
Alan M. Baum and Donald J. McMillan, *General Motors Research Laboratory*

SIMULATION ENVIRONMENTS AND TOOLS

New tools and programmer interfaces for concurrent discrete event simulation are presented.

The Yaddes distributed discrete event simulation specification language and execution environments
Bruno R. Preiss, *University of Waterloo*

Tools for measuring the performance and diagnosing the behavior of distributed simulations using time warp
Steven Bellenot, *The Florida State University,* Michael Di Loreto, *California Institute of Technology*

An interface for programming parallel simulations
D. H. Gill, F. X. Maginnis, S. R. Rainer and T. P. Reagan, *The MITRE Corporation*

SIMULATION OF LOGIC CIRCUITS

New ideas regarding parallel simulation of digital hardware using general purpose and special purpose computers are presented.

The effect of timing on the parallelism available for parallel circuit simulation
Mary Bailey and Lawrence Snyder, *University of Washington*

A multi-transputer-net as a logic simulation environment
Winfried Hahn, Herbert Anger, Andreas Hagerer and Bernd Schuster, *University of Passau*

An accelerator for time driven logic simulation
H. M. Thaker and W. M. Loucks, *University of Waterloo*

A structural mapping for parallel digital logic simulation
Mark Davoren, *University of Edinburgh*

APPLICATIONS

Performance evaluations and techniques for concurrent simulation in specific application areas are discussed.

Tailoring a parallel trace-driven simulation technique to specific multiprocessor cache coherence protocols
Yi-Bing Lin, Jean-Loup Baer and Edward D. Lazowska, *University of Washington*

Time-driven parallel simulation of multistage interconnection networks
Qing Yu and Don Towsley, University of Massachusetts, Philip Heidelberger, *IBM Research Division*

Mixed event — and time-stepped parallel simulation
David W. O'Brien and John B. Gilmer, *The BDM Corporation*

PANEL SESSION

Future directions in concurrent simulation. Where will we be five years from now? Panel members present their views of the most important future research directions in parallel and distributed discrete event simulation. After a brief 5 minute position statement by each panel member, the audience is invited to question the panel.

MODERATOR: Richard M. Fujimoto, *University of Utah*
PANEL MEMBERS: TBA

19

MICHAEL DI LORETO

CHAPTER 21

1979 - 1989

Merrie Computing Company

WHEN I STARTED at JPL in 1979, I was an Independent Consultant. I worked for myself. However, JPL would not make a contract with a person. They only dealt with corporations. I had to join a contracting company as a sub-contractor, and they took a quarter of my money! That was no good, so in 1980 Martin Orton and I formed our own California corporation to get our own money back. I mentioned he was from England. He also had an English sense of humor. At Christmas time he would answer the phone or just say to people *"Merry Computing!"* So, his being British, *Merrie Computing Company* became the name of our corporation. He was the President because he wanted to be, and I was the Vice President because I didn't care. Actually, he was senior to me, it was his idea, and he did all the work to set up the corporation. We split the other corporate titles, like Secretary and Treasurer. I was the Chief Scientist.

We succeeded in getting contracts for ourselves and everything was going well. We weren't splitting our paychecks with anyone else. We were also allowed to charge JPL for our business overhead, which had no limit, but ours was very small. Then, because we had our contracting business all set up, we were able to get jobs at JPL for other people who were Independent Consultants like we had been. It was a good deal for everyone. Because of our low overhead, JPL could pay less for better Programmers, they could get paid more, and we got a little bit too. We eventually had a lot of people working for our company. We even rented a real office and hired a full-time manager to handle invoicing, paying people, and so on. This went on for 10 years.

In 1989, JPL declined to renew our contract. They said the government wanted to have disadvantaged minority-run small businesses. They also said that they thought it was risky to do business with a small company whose only customer was JPL. They didn't seem to get the irony of putting us out of business for that reason. There were other small contracting companies like ours. We had actually benefited from their getting rid of some of our competitors when they wanted woman-owned businesses. When that happened, the people who worked at JPL stayed on the same job, but had to switch contracting companies. They often came to us, and we had as many as 40 people at one point.

When our contract ended, all of our people had to switch to other companies. I remember a little about one of the companies because they tried to recruit me. To me, they were a big company, but the government's definition of a small business was up to 400 employees. The president of the company was from Korea, so that made it a minority-run business. But it didn't give minority people jobs. The same contractors who were already there just had to switch to the new company. Their corporate headquarters were in Washington, D.C., all the better for lobbying for government contracts. Our idea was that a local company with low overhead and a record of good service was not only good for us, but good for JPL too. We were easy to deal with and we charged less money. I mentioned that overhead was unlimited. It just depended on the company's expenses, which included offices, utilities, equipment, salaries, travel, and anything else you could think of. Of course, that company's overhead was a lot more than ours was. The government doesn't care if they pay more. It's not their money. Not bitter. It was good while it lasted.

CHAPTER 22

1989 - 1990

Jade Simulations International

S O, I HAD to leave JPL. I got a contract with a company in Calgary, Alberta, Canada called Jade Simulations International. They had their own TimeWarp operating system and a simulation system they called SIM++. Their software was written in C++, and one of the things they wanted me to do was to port the C++ compiler to the SUN4. At that time, the C++ compiler was a pre-processor to the C language. It was called Cfront. I also developed object-oriented TimeWarp Execution Analysis Tools (TWEAT) in C++ with SunView and X Windows. I worked there for about 3 months, traveling there for a week or two at a time from my home in Diamond Bar, CA.

The president of Jade Simulations was Brian Unger. He was from the University of Calgary, and he was the conference chair for that Distributed Simulation Conference in Florida that I mentioned earlier. I was referred to him by Dave Jefferson, the Computer Science professor from UCLA who was the Principle Investigator of our TimeWarp project at JPL. At the end of my contract, Brian offered me a full-time job there. He paid for my wife and me to travel to Calgary and he personally took us around looking at houses. It was very tempting. I liked the company, the job, the people who worked there, and I liked him. It was tough, but I ended up not taking it.

Now there's a gap in my time line. This is 2024 and I'm trying to remember what happened in 1990. I always used to put every job I had on my resumé, but it got to be very long. People said that a resumé should be 1 or 2 pages long, and should not go back more than 10 years. I did that for my own history because I really liked all the things I did. Eventually I started making shorter ones. I also made one that was a 1-page summary and other short ones that were targeted at specific jobs. My last full resumé from 2017 is only 6 pages. It wasn't easy, but I managed to find an old resumé from 2009 that had all my jobs back to the beginning. But there are still a few months missing between January, 1990 when I left Jade Simulations, and May of that year.

I remember now that at about that time I joined an Earthwatch archaeological project in Ghana, and it just so happened that the head archaeologist was from the university in Calgary. He was already in Ghana, but he had forgotten to take his favorite trowel, so he asked me to get it for him. I went to the university, got his trowel, and took it with me. I couldn't carry it on the plane, though. I had to be checked in its own box like a weapon, which I guess it could be in the wrong hands. My mission was a success. I arrived in Accra with the trowel safely in hand, and delivered it to the archaeologist. That accounts for at least 3 weeks in early 1990.

It's good to have a purpose. I've always thought from my first job that my purpose was to develop software or solve problems for someone, to help them do something they want to do or to get something they want. I often think of programming as performing a service. It's very satisfying to accomplish something for another person. This should count as a programming lesson.

CHAPTER 23

May - December 1990

JPL - European Command

I N MAY OF 1990 I went back to JPL. My contract was held by one of the few remaining local companies which was officially woman-owned. The owner of the company was a guy Martin and I knew, and he cleverly listed his wife as co-owner and didn't go out of business like we did. It was okay. Sorry I don't remember their names. I think the woman actually did run their office.

When I went to an interview for my next job at JPL, the manager told me, "*You have a reputation for saving projects.*" I didn't know that, but I knew she was talking about the JTLS and TimeWarp projects, both of which were doomed until I got them working. So, it wasn't much of an interview. She just hired me right away.

The project was for the European Command of the U.S. Military. I designed and implemented the EUCOM Decision Support System (EDSS) applications database management support software in ADA with SYBASE, SQL and UNIX on DECstation 3100 computers. I installed both Commercial and Secure SYBASE on the VAX 6420 with ULTRIX.

I also designed and implemented the DBATOOL program in ADA with MOTIF and X Windows. This was a general purpose relational database access and display program with interactive forms generation and editing. I also used the Rational ADA development system.

This was not one of my better projects. As you can see, I did some very interesting technical things, but I was very critical of the management and organization. The manager wanted us to estimate the number of lines of code we were going to write each week, and then at the end of the week count the number of lines of code and compare the two. That was supposed to measure progress. That kind of thing does not make sense at all to a Programmer. As for the organization, I was a sub-contractor to a small contracting company. But naturally, the government wanted a big contracting company to manage the project. So the contracting company I worked for contracted to that bigger company, TRW, I think. They in turn had a contract with the government. I had no way to know, but, by the time you went through all those layers of contracting, I wouldn't be surprised if my hourly rate was as much as $500/hr, about 10 times what I got.

From about August of 1990 to December of that year, at the same time as I was at JPL on the EUCOM project, I had another job with Input Systems, Inc. in Paramount, CA. I did COBOL programming on an IBM 4341 with OS/VS1. And I converted software to MicroFocus COBOL and Microsoft BASIC for an IBM PC with MS-DOS and Novell Datatrieve.

CHAPTER 24

1991 - 1992

JPL - TOPEX / Poseidon Satellite

I N JANUARY OF 1991, until August of 1992, I worked at JPL on the Telemetry Command and Communications Subsystem (TCCS) for the TOPEX/Poseidon satellite. I was on a team of 4 or 5 Programmers developing the TCCS User Interface using C, Smartstar and DEC RDB (Relational Database). I also on my own developed software in C and SCHEME on the VAX 6410 with VMS for testing the NASA Communications Network (NASCOM) Front End Processor (NFEP). I was hired for this job by Mike DeGyurky, my previous manager from the JTLS project.

This project had its faults, but it was really good. JPL built their own Mission Control Center in a building on campus that was like what you would see in a movie, except smaller. There was a good-size room with several workstations where the mission operators could control the TOPEX/Poseidon satellite. That satellite measured the surface height of the ocean which, apparently varies quite a lot. They could see streams and rivers on the surface of the ocean.

The silly part to me was the idea that, *"All the documentation should be done before the first line of code."* If you're a Programmer, you know that's stupid. However, it seemed to reflect a trend in software project management. They also had the idea of counting lines of code. I talked a little before about how, when I got on a project, I would organize and generally clean up the software. At Aeronutronic Ford, as System Integrator I took the other Programmers' code and fixed it up to the point of almost rewriting it. I did the same thing when I joined the TimeWarp project. I was doing something similar for the TCCS User Interface software.

One day, one of my co-workers was joking with me saying something like, *"You're hurting our code count. When you work on it you make negative lines of code."* And so I did. When I found duplicated code, I reorganized it into subroutines. I don't really think the other Programmers did that on purpose to have more lines of code, but it almost looked that way. More likely they were just copying and pasting code in a hurry.

There was still no Internet yet. The NASA Communications Network (NASCOM) was the way they communicated between their various centers, like Houston, Goddard and JPL. Data from the TOPEX/Poseidon satellite went to another communications satellite, and from there to Goddard Space Flight Center in Maryland. From there it went to JPL by NASCOM. To handle the communications, we had a NASCOM Front End Processor (NFEP) that was connected to the network and to the VAX. This NFEP was a new thing and I was given the task of testing it.

I said there was no Internet, but, since the early 1980's there was the Ethernet. Our Sun workstations on the TimeWarp project were connected to each other that way. The TCP/IP protocol that was used for communicating between computers on an Ethernet was invented by Sun. My test program ran on the VAX and communicated with the NFEP by TCP/IP. While I was working on it, I discovered something wrong. The purpose of testing is to find something wrong, so that was a good thing in a way. The communication between the two machines was failing. It was pretty difficult to find out why, and I resorted to using a tool that could record TCP/IP traffic. The TCP/IP protocol is well documented, but it turned out there was a kind of loop hole where some small detail could be interpreted in more than one way, but still comply with the protocol. In this case, I found out that the way the two machines handled "sliding windows" was slightly different and sometimes failed. I pinned it down and submitted a bug to DEC with a clear trace of the message traffic. They accepted it as a real bug on their part and soon fixed it.

MICHAEL DI LORETO

SCHEME is a very small dialect of LISP written in C. I started out working in C, but somebody recommended that I try the SCHEME language. It seems to me it was Brian Beckman, but I can't be sure because he was already long gone to Microsoft. We were still in touch, though, so it's possible. He even recommended me for a job there, but I failed the interview.

I liked SCHEME. Not only was it a new language for me, but it worked really well for what I was trying to do, which was to develop a test system with a graphical user interface.

There was an actual LISP Machine in a small room with a chair that I could play with as well because, of course, JPL had everything.

While I was with that group at JPL, I also did some other small jobs. I developed an optical disk archive utility in INGRES QUEL for the Alaska SAR. I organized and recoded the tape recording task (SPODR) for the JPL Ground Communications Facility (GCF) on a MODCOMP computer with REAL/IX. That's all I know. If it weren't for my old resumé I wouldn't have remembered them at all.

The National Aeronautics and Space Administration

Presents the

GROUP ACHIEVEMENT AWARD

for the

TOPEX/POSEIDON Ground Data System

to

Michael DiLoreto

Telemetry, Command, and Communications Subsystem

in recognition of outstanding achievement in the design, development, test, and operations of the TOPEX/POSEIDON ground operations system.

Signed and sealed at Washington, D.C.
this tenth day of February
nineteen hundred and ninety-three

Daniel S. Goldin, Administrator, NASA

Since I mentioned Brian Beckman and Microsoft, I have to say a few more things about both of them. I called Brian a genius and I meant it. For his own interest, he memorized the Koran, and he could recite it in an authentic Arabic accent. Of course, not knowing Arabic, I can't really verify his accent or if his recital was correct. It's just that he was so good I didn't ever doubt it. One time at work on the TimeWarp project we happened to be sitting together in a room chatting. He proposed we play a game that was that one of us would open an English dictionary at random and stick a finger in it without looking, and then say the word to the other player, who would attempt to tell what its definition was. I thought I could do that. I'm very smart, I read a lot of books, and I think my vocabulary is better than average. To my dismay, though, the words he picked without looking were words I'd never heard of or could even guess. I couldn't really do it. He, on the other hand, knew the definition of every word I picked. So, obviously, he was way smarter than me. I think maybe he read the whole dictionary in advance and memorized all the words. That's not fair, is it? Maybe not, but it's a sign of a really high IQ.

One day Brian and I were having a technical discussion. It might even have been the same time as the game I just mentioned because my memory has us in the same place. Anyway, we were disagreeing about something, I don't know what about, Object-Oriented Programming or Database Management or whatever, and he got frustrated and told me, "*Since you didn't go to college, you were never trained to think correctly!*" I didn't reply. That was the end of the discussion. But I thought to myself, "*That's right. I never was trained to think correctly.*"

I think the way I think just naturally. I was never institutionalized or indoctrinated by anyone. Even my parents didn't try to teach me anything or discipline me. I think it was normal at the time when I was a child, the 1950s, for children to be fed and taken care of, but then left on their own to grow up. We were like the kids in the Peanuts comic strip who had their own lives with no parents around. Whatever discipline I had was just from myself, and pretty much everything I know about computers and software I taught myself. I consider myself fortunate not to have had to go to kindergarten or preschool or day care. I started school in the first grade, and I only learned to read and do arithmetic after that. I'm really sorry for kids now that have all that pressure to learn academic things right from when they are born.

I didn't want to call that discussion with Brian an argument because I wanted to explain what I think an argument is. To me, the purpose of an argument about a technical issue is to find the right answer. You exchange ideas in order to discover the truth. You give and take. If the other person says something that makes sense, you agree. The other purpose of an argument is to win. You maintain your position at all costs, and reject anything from your opponent. When Brian talked about training to think correctly, I took it that that's what he meant. That in college you're trained to win arguments. I think that's what rhetoric is, and I have a very negative view of it. My discomfort with the way Brian was arguing was that it seemed to me he was using a technique that involved the shifting of the meanings of words. The way that works is that you can say one thing is just like another thing that is really not the same by manipulating the definitions of words to get to the point where you can claim there's no difference between the two things. I don't like it because you're not trying to reach an honest conclusion, you're just trying to win. And Brian was absolutely correct in saying that I was not trained to think that way. I'm glad I wasn't.

There's something unique about being a Computer Programmer. In any other profession where you deal with people, you can always argue that you're right even when you're wrong. You never have to give up. You can make excuses, blame other people, deny that something is the case, and insist that your position is correct no matter what. Programmers can't do that. I used to say to myself, *"No matter how smart you think you are, the computer can always prove you're wrong."*

If your program doesn't work, you can't argue with the computer. You can't claim that the program really did work in spite of what the computer says. Except for rare occasions, the computer is always right. Blaming the computer or someone else won't make your program work. The only way to make your program work is to admit you made a mistake and try to find out what it is. Then you can correct it. Being a Programmer takes a humility that others don't have to have. That same attitude also makes me say, *"I'm never 100% sure of anything."*

I think the reason I was so much better at solving computer problems than most others was that I was dedicated to finding the truth wherever it was. I didn't deny that the problem exists even if it was caused by my own mistake. I just analyzed the situation and went to where the problem was wherever it was. Being a Programmer means you have to know that you make mistakes. You can't always be right. I would even say a Programmer's job is to make mistakes. I think I remember seeing a poster on the wall of an office there at JPL with a picture of Albert Einstein and a caption that said, *"He who never makes a mistake never makes anything."* I can't vouch for that quotation or even if Einstein said it, but I wholly agree with the sentiment.

Here's something I learned about making mistakes. If you know you're going to make mistakes in your program, the logical thing to do is to try to minimize those mistakes, and try to minimize the effort it will take to find and fix the mistakes. This is another lesson

MICHAEL DI LORETO

in programming, but I suppose it could be used in other fields as well. With this in mind, I deliberately tried to design software so that it would be easier to understand and easier to change. So much software is so fragile that changing anything can break it. Software has a really bad reputation because of that.

Brian Beckman had some very high technical position at Microsoft in Redmond, which was only natural for someone like him. And he thought enough of me to recommend me for a job there. His influence was such that they agreed to interview me. I traveled there the night before and I called to tell him I was there and ready for the interview. He said, *"Don't wear a suit."* I said, *"Too late. That's what I brought to wear."* I had been wearing a suit and tie and carrying a briefcase every day since I started working in 1968. I eventually gave it up some time after I started working at JPL because the place was like a college campus and the workers all wore t-shirts and jeans. Only the managers and I wore a suit. But the long walk from the parking lot to the office building in the hot Summer sun finally convinced me to do what everyone else there did. However, when I went to other companies, I wanted to present myself as a professional, so I still wore a suit on those occasions. Well, that was strike one. The people at Microsoft didn't like suits.

In the old days, I would have an interview with a manager, and he or she would hire me, or not. At some point, though, it became a thing for members of the staff to interview a new candidate. That didn't work out well for me and I'll say more about this later. My interview at Microsoft was with several different people, but not for the same reason. At Brian's recommendation, they were considering hiring me without any particular job in mind, and then, once hired, they would find a place for me. On the other hand, maybe that's how they hired everybody. I think most of the interviews were okay, except for me looking so strange in my suit, but there was one I remember that must have been the one that sunk me. The guy had written some problem on the white board in his office and he asked me to solve it. I didn't even try to do it. It's not because it was too hard. It was just that I was in "professional" mode and not in "problem solving" mode. I don't know if anyone can relate to that.

Whenever I visited a company as an Independent Consultant, I would talk to the manager or the president of the company on their level. I would get the information about what they wanted to have done, make a deal, and go away. When I was alone later I would work on the project, solving whatever problems there were. To me, those were two distinctly different activities. In that interview, I was perfectly willing to take his problem and go away and solve it, but that's not what he wanted. He said he wanted to see how I think. Well, the way I think is by sitting by myself and thinking, not by standing in front of a white board and talking. Did he see that? Nah.

Now I wonder if it's even possible to see how someone else thinks. I'm skeptical. What if you just ask them? You might find out if they think the same way you do because that might be understandable. But what if they think some other way you're not familiar with? Oh, well.

I told that stupid story because I thought there might be a lesson in it. The lesson is that different people don't all think the same way. They're not right or wrong, just different. It used to be that Programmers were known to be asocial. I even knew a Programmer once who called himself that, and I agreed with it right away. Programming is not a social activity. It's why some very smart people who want to be Programmers can't stand it. It's mostly sitting by yourself working on puzzles. Did you notice in my descriptions how many of my jobs involved me sitting in some small room, or sometimes a bigger room, with just a computer and no one else? That's what Programming is like. It seems the younger generations now like to work in groups, standing in front of a white board and talking. I guess that must be good for them. They seem to be very successful. In my experience, though, I've never seen a real problem solved by talking about it. Well, that's just my experience. It's not everything.

CHAPTER 25

1992 - 1994

JPL - Cassini Spacecraft ISS

F ROM SEPTEMBER, 1992 to November, 1994 I worked on the Cassini Mission to Saturn. I designed and implemented the Electronic Ground Support Equipment (EGSE) software for the Imaging Science Subsystem (ISS) which is an instrument on the Cassini Spacecraft. Actually, there are two of them: one with a narrow angle camera and the other one with a wide angle camera. I used C++ with TCP/IP and X Windows on a Sun SPARCstation. The EGSE parses and sends commands to the flight computer; receives, logs and displays telemetry in real time; controls and monitors the instrument power; decompresses, processes and displays images; and can simulate science and housekeeping data for EGSE software testing.

The EGSE software is an open client-server architecture of my own invention, and consists of over a dozen cooperating independent programs, each with its own Graphical User Interface. The programs communicate with each other by TCP/IP, with ports dynamically allocated by a "master" server, and can run on a network of separate computers if desired.

I also designed and implemented the ISS Bench Checkout Equipment (BCE) software in ADA for the IBM MIL-STD 1750A Engineering Flight Computer (EFC). This software receives and executes the same commands as the flight software; operates all the hardware devices; takes pictures with the CCD camera; and transmits science and housekeeping data. This completely emulates the flight software for the purposes of testing the new flight computer hardware, debugging the EGSE software, and prototyping techniques which were used by the flight software.

I also developed the ISS Startup ROM software in 1750A Assembler Language. This program initializes and self-tests the EFC, loads flight software from the spacecraft Central Data System (CDS), and exercises the shutter and filter wheels without the flight software for diagnostic and maintenance purposes. It is used in flight.

I also integrated the GSE (ground) and BCE (flight) systems with an RTIU (CDS simulator) to make a complete end-to-end system, and used it to help the electronics engineers test and debug the new imaging system hardware. This resulted in a fully functional and reliable system ready for unobstructed flight software development.

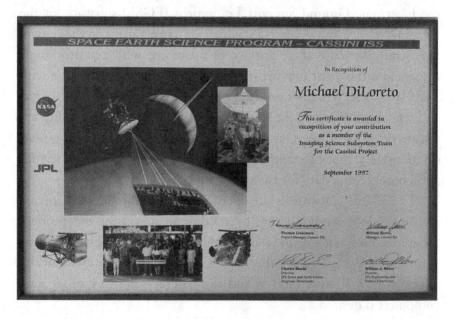

The last five paragraphs are pretty much what I wrote in my resumé for the Cassini project. That's why they sound so stiff, and not in keeping with my story telling style. I think this might have been my most significant development project. All those things I just mentioned were done entirely by me alone. I was given a Sun SPARCstation with the Solaris operating system, but I selected the C++ language and X

Windows and the UNIX System V Transport Layer Interface (TLI) for inter-process communication by TCP/IP. Then I used Sun's DevGuide GUI builder to create all the programs.

I talked before about another Ground Support Equipment (GSE) system I created before for an instrument on the CRRES satellite. Before I say more, I should explain that an "instrument" is a computer system that is on board a satellite or spacecraft. A satellite, of course, orbits the Earth, while a spacecraft travels to other planets. The Cassini spacecraft has, as I said, a Central Data System (CDS) and fourteen instruments, two of which are the imaging systems. Each instrument was a separate project to develop the hardware and software to do whatever it does. I don't know, but I think it's possible that some instruments may be developed outside of JPL.

I was part of the project to build the instrument known as the Imaging Science Subsystem (ISS). There were maybe 10 or 12 people altogether in our own office space, and we had our own clean room lab. We wore those white anti-static lab coats like you see scientists wear in movies. The ISS instrument had a CCD camera and a power system that was built by electronics engineers in the group. It also had a JPEG compressor chip to make the images smaller for transmission.

The whole purpose of a Ground Support Equipment (GSE) system is to test an instrument. This always seemed like a very good idea to me. When JPL had a project to build a space instrument, they also included another whole project to build a test system for it. I myself had been using a similar technique for my own projects. I used to say, "*When you write a program, plan on writing three more to test it.*" I also used to say, "*Don't schedule more than 50% of your time.*"

Sorry about the digression, but I think those two things I just said are very important principles of software projects, and you've never heard them before because no one else follows them. When I said to write three more programs, I didn't necessarily mean exactly three. The idea is that, in order to test a new program, you're likely to need another one to generate test data (input), another one to execute the test (process), and another one or more to analyze the results (output). You know already that programs pretty much always have input, processing and output (IPO).

The reason major projects fail is that they suffer from the Mythical Man-Month syndrome. Simply put, you have some estimate of the number of lines of code that are going to be needed, you have some amount of time for the project to be done, often dictated by whoever is paying for it, and you have some idea of how many lines of code a Programmer can produce in a month. Then, a simple calculation tells you how many people you need. I would have to read *The Mythical Man-Month* again to see if that's what it says. This is just my version of it.

One of the symptoms of this syndrome, or misunderstanding, is that managers get the idea that they can make a schedule based on man hours that they get from having Programmers estimate how long they think some particular programming task will take. Sometimes they realize there's something wrong with that idea, and say they want the estimates in "engineering hours". That's to allow for the fact that people don't work 100% of the time on the task assigned to them. But then they turn those engineering hours into calendar time, and they're behind schedule right from the start. They never even try to estimate the time people spend in meetings, for example. My 50% rule of thumb came to me because of projects like that.

So, the way JPL would set up a full-scale project to develop a test system always impressed me. The GSE is just used for development testing. When the spacecraft is in flight, they have a ground system for sending commands, receiving telemetry and images, recording, displaying, and so on. The GSE does something that's a lot like what the real ground system does. Isn't that redundant? Couldn't they just use the ground system to test the flight instruments? They could, but it's a much smarter approach to build separate test systems. To me, it's analogous to my write three more programs idea. Why do that? When the program is really in use, it gets tested then, right? The answer depends on what you think testing is.

There used to be a management view of software development called the Waterfall Model. Essentially, a software project had three phases: design, code, test. They imagined that there was a design phase and, when that was done, an implementation phase (coding), and finally a testing phase. I have no idea how they saw that as something falling down, but it was a serious project planning and scheduling methodology in the 1980s. I don't believe any real Programmers ever thought that made sense. We mostly just ignored it and did what we knew how to do. Hopefully, management techniques like that are long gone, but probably not.

The testing part of the project was that, when the code was all written, you ran it to see if it worked. More specifically, you ran the program to show that it *does* work. This is what I was getting at by saying it depends on what you think testing is. Either the purpose of the test is to demonstrate that the program is working correctly, or its purpose is to find something wrong. There's a big difference. For example, there is time scheduled for testing, but no time for fixing things that are wrong. Creating test tools is something that Programmers do, but don't talk about. That kind of activity is not estimated or scheduled. It's just some kind of overhead.

When I started out, a fundamental concept was program design. I learned that a program is designed first and then coded. Then, of course, the program is tested. That doesn't sound too far off from that Waterfall Model, does it? I suppose it was probably a reasonable concept when it was first proposed, but then got formalized into ridiculousness. Now the whole thing is backwards. There's something called test-driven development where a test is written first, and then the code is written to pass the test. The design part is apparently just gone.

I used to say, *"My program works by design"*. To me, that meant I knew the program was going to work before I wrote it. If I made mistakes in coding, there would be bugs, but they would not be fatal. I would quickly fix the bugs and the program would be done. I've seen too much software that was produced by coding something that was approximately what the Programmers thought it should be, and then debugging it until it worked. In many cases, that never ends. There are always more bugs. I would say, *"That program works by luck."*

When I designed a program, I would also design a way to test it. That would include those extra three programs, naturally, but often it would be some way in the program to directly observe what it was doing. I called that instrumentation because of the way I could see everything that the program did. Most of the things any program does are invisible. You only see the final results. Normally, people judge whether the results are correct or not and, if not, then they go into a debugging mode to try to find out what went wrong. I call that negative debugging. You're working backwards from some wrong result to try to find the source of it. I say my approach is positive because my built-in instrumentation shows me exactly what happens at every step of the code's execution. It looks like a nice trace of all the steps. It positively proves the code is right.

I talked before about how sometimes I went way out of the way to design a whole new language just for the application I was hired to do. I claimed that, by spending more time designing, I spent a lot less time debugging. The program instrumentation I just described is another thing that takes significant time up front, but makes testing so much easier that the development time is far less overall. I don't think anybody ever measures debugging time. In the Waterfall Model, it comes after the design-code-test phases are done. You're now on unscheduled time, and it's a very frustrating part of a project. It seems endless. It's when the project succeeds or fails.

I think one of my specialties was debugging. I was really good at it. I've said how I always finished my projects on time, and always had time to help others. I think that's both due to finding and fixing bugs very quickly, but also to just creating a lot fewer bugs in the first place. The techniques I've described prevent bugs. I'll have more to say about "*Debugging Science*".

I was bragging about how JPL would set up whole projects to build test systems for instruments. It may sound like a lot of bureaucracy, but for the ones I worked on, the whole project was just me, and I could do whatever I wanted. I conceived of the GSE as a series of independent programs that had a Graphical User Interface and could communicate. Each program could be a client and a server. For example, the program that received telemetry from the instrument would record it and then make it available to other programs as a service. Another program that wants to display the data could connect to the server as a client to receive the data. There were two kinds of telemetry data, housekeeping and images. Housekeeping is basically just numbers indicating the state of the instrument. Images are pictures of Saturn. Different programs were clients of the different kinds of telemetry. The housekeeping display program did just that, displayed housekeeping data. An image processing program decompressed and displayed pictures. I invented a way to dynamically allocate TCP/IP ports so there could be an unlimited number of programs.

Sun had a great program called OpenWindows Developer's Guide, or DevGuide. It had a graphical user interface that could be used to create a graphical user interface. I would put graphical widgets on the screen like buttons, labels, text boxes, and so on, and then the DevGuide would actually generate a C program with the new GUI and stubs for the action routines, like a button press, for example. Then I would edit the program and insert my own code to handle the actions. Best of all, and I was very particular about this, after I modified the code, I could use the DevGuide to change the GUI and it would generate new code, which it would then merge with my own code! I can't tell you how cool that was. If it couldn't merge right, I wouldn't have use it.

Now you probably want to know how to test a test system. It's software that needs testing too. We had a machine in our lab called Bench Checkout Equipment (BCE). This included a 1750A flight computer and interfaces to the camera and other devices. Instruments on the Cassini spacecraft communicate with a Central Data System (CDS) which communicates with the ground. We also had another machine called an RTIU which was a CDS simulator. From my GSE, I had a way to communicate through the RTIU to the ISS flight computer.

So, to test the GSE, I wrote a program in ADA for the 1750A. ADA was originally designed for flight computers, and it can run on a bare machine with no operating system. You can write code to do I/O and handle interrupts all in ADA without having to go into machine code. I made that program receive commands from the GSE and send telemetry to the GSE.

The electronics designer, my good friend, Perry, used some design tool to create his design, then workers in the lab implemented it doing the wiring on the board by hand. It was called wire wrapping. He then used an oscilloscope to debug the electronics. This board controlled the instrument's devices, like the camera, and was interfaced to the computer. Therefore, I helped him by writing ADA code to interact with the electronics board. For example, to test some component on the board, I would program the computer to do some I/O to the board, and then Perry would watch what it did on the oscilloscope. If my program could also read something from the board, that would help too. I spent a lot of time in the lab with Perry helping to test and debug the electronics. For awhile, we were working together all day every day.

I like to say I helped the electronics engineer debug his board because I think it was an extra contribution I made to the project beyond my assignment. I can't say I could read a schematic diagram, but I had some experience looking at them before when I was working on the Real-Time Combiner, and I completely understood digital logic. I would say, *"Logic is my business."* We had to discuss the electronics in order for me to construct tests on the computer. When he explained what he saw on the oscilloscope, I could help reason about what it meant. That would lead to my changing my ADA program to refine the test. It was like an evolving diagnostic test program. It didn't just test working hardware, it was a tool for debugging it. This collaboration between hardware and software was very effective and also very enjoyable.

Eventually, the electronics board was working well enough that my ADA program could make it operate all the devices, including the ultimate goal of taking pictures. The same program could also receive commands from the GSE and send data back. Sitting in the lab at a Sun workstation, I could click a button on the graphical user interface of one of my programs, it would send a command to the BCE where my ADA program was running, it would make the camera take a picture and send the image back to the GSE where another of my programs would display it.

When visitors came to tour our lab, I would have them sit on a chair in front of the camera and take their picture. Then I would print it and give it to them as a souvenir. They liked it, but the CCD camera was way too sensitive to take pictures of people. It showed the veins under their skin, which was not really that attractive.

Debugging was a very important part of what I did in just about all my jobs. A little while ago I made up the term *"Debugging Science"*. That's not a real thing. In general, it seems that debugging is not taken very seriously. Have you ever read a book about it before? I've talked a lot about my debugging philosophy. I've tried to point out how having a disciplined approach to problem solving gets much better results than the usual guess-work. I described my not really famous, not really patented two-step methodology. I just now went into how this approach works not just for software, but for electronics as well.

I didn't go to college. I began my programming career at 18. I gained a lot of experience, and I was very good at what I did. But I always thought that people with Computer Science degrees would pass me up. They never did. One possible explanation, I thought, was that they didn't teach debugging in college. Even someone with a PhD in Computer Science could not do what I did. I attributed that to experience. I said how I used all my experience even from computers that you never heard of to solve problems. That was real experience solving real problems. By helping other people with their problems, I gained even more experience with even more different things.

Experience is normally measured in numbers of years. Someone with 5 to 10 years of experience could call themselves a Senior Software Engineer. However, that was often several years of experience on the same job. I considered myself extremely fortunate to have so many different jobs in a relatively short amount of time. It's often hard for a Programmer to get a job doing something they had not done before. For my first several years, either by the companies going out of business or by getting layed off or fired, I had a totally different kind of job every year, and in each one I learned new computers and programming languages.

On the other hand, there were two other computer pioneers who also didn't finish college, Steve Jobs and Bill Gates. That makes three of us. Ha ha. But they both graduated from high school and went to college at least for awhile. It's interesting they were both the same age, born in 1955, five years after me. They both started with computers later than me, although Bill Gates began programming at an earlier age. I don't know if Steve Jobs did programming at all. Obviously, it's ridiculous to compare myself to either of them. They're both geniuses and I'm not. Sometimes I'm a little defensive about being uneducated, but then I'm also kind of proud of it.

Sometimes we use 'debugging' and 'troubleshooting' interchangeably. I also refer to them both as 'problem solving'. What's the difference? Thinking about it now, I would say that debugging is what a Programmer normally does when they've written some new code. Mistakes are inevitable. There are always bugs in new code. Finding and fixing them is a routine part of the programming process. It's when a working system fails that I call finding and fixing the problem 'troubleshooting'. It's like what I called 'negative debugging', working backwards from some error to what caused it. For me, that was almost always other people's programs, but I can remember one time where a system I designed and built had a failure after it was put into use. That was the database management system I created for Infodetics. I can't remember what happened now, except that it was some rare condition that was hard to track down. Martin Orton helped me with it, which was pretty unusual since I was always the one helping other people. That is, other people but not him. I don't think he ever needed my help. He was ahead of me.

What makes some failures so difficult to diagnose is that they are timing related. That is, a normally working system will run into some unexpected condition that depends on the timing of events. That kind of failure is pretty much always intermittent. You can't predict when the failure is going to happen. Some failures happen often, others once a day, once a month, or even once a year. The more often it happens, the easier it is to track it down.

The standard way to work on any failure is to reproduce the problem. That might mean just running the program again and seeing it fail again. If the problem repeats, the next thing to do is to run the program with an interactive debugger. Some errors will automatically cause control to be transferred to the debugger. Then you can see the state of the program at the point of failure. For example, an access violation interrupts the program on the instruction that caused it. That does not necessarily mean that that instruction was wrong, probably not. It's more likely the conditions leading up to it that resulted in a faulty address that the instruction happened to use.

I said before how many Programmers guess what's wrong and change something to see if the problem goes away. That's what I mocked as the one-step technique. I also referred to the *printf* fix without explaining what it was. Another way Programmers try to find out what caused a failure is to insert print statements into the code to get more information. In the C language, *printf* is the statement you use to print things. Sometimes, especially for timing related problems, adding a print statement makes the problem go away because it changes the timing. I generalize that to say that the effect of changing any code might make a problem go away for the same reason. This is what's wrong with the one-step guessing technique. The problem may go away, but it may not really be fixed. It might just happen less often, but the Programmer can claim to have fixed it.

My approach is exactly the opposite. I don't want a bug to go away or happen less often. Whatever I do to the code to isolate the problem, I always want the bug to keep happening. I'm very careful to not let a bug get away or go into hiding. If a bug gets lost, you can't fix it. It's a very delicate balance to make changes to the code without changing any of the conditions. Of course, you can't use a breakpoint to catch something that happens one in a million times. And, as I said, printing things can change the timing and cover up the bug.

What I really want to do is make the failure happen *more* often. If it can be made to happen every time, for example, it may continue to happen even with print statements, and a breakpoint in the debugger might catch it. Doing this is not really as easy as it sounds. It takes experience, know-how, and even some creativity. The goal is to definitively prove the cause of the problem. The exact conditions that led to the failure have to be explained. Once the true cause of a problem is understood, the path to fixing it is usually straightforward. There's no guessing. You know what's wrong and why it's wrong. This explanation may seem a little circular because changing the code to make a failure happen more often involves trial and error, or, in other words, guessing.

You're not guessing the answer, though. You hypothesize what the trouble might be, and then experiment with ways to prove it. And the hypothesis is not just picking something out of the air. It's based on years of experience solving other more or less similar problems. You don't know what caused the failure, but you do know what kinds of things cause failures like that.

CHAPTER 26

1994 - 1995

NASA Jet Propulsion Laboratory

I N NOVEMBER OF 1994, I left the Cassini ISS project. I think my work was just about all done, but I was having trouble with the manager. I don't remember exactly what it was, but generally when a manager thinks he knows my job better than I do, we don't get along. It's bad when a manager thinks he's the system designer. To me, the best managers are the ones who leave me alone to do what I do. Blame me, if you want. Anyway, I joined a supercomputer group. I had access to a Cray machine, and I tinkered with it a little, but not very much.

I worked on the SGI Flight Simulator program to make it communicate with other simulators such as the JPL Advanced Simulation Framework, using the proposed IEEE standard protocol for Distributed Interactive Simulations (DIS). The idea of that was to have a human-operated simulation interact in real time with a computer-generated simulation in a standard way, in effect, merging the virtual worlds of otherwise independent simulations.

When I was working on the TimeWarp project, Leo Blume was part of the team. I had TimeWarp working on the VAX, the Mark II HyperCube, the Mark III Hypercube, the network of Sun workstations, and the BBN Butterfly multiprocessor. The machine I didn't work on was the Transputer. Leo was doing that. I didn't have anything to do with it other than I think I helped him with some small problem one time.

Leo Blume left JPL to go to work at Silicon Graphics, Inc. (SGI) in Mountain View, CA. That company was the hottest startup in Silicon

Valley. Their machines were used to do computer graphics for movies like Star Wars. He was a Programmer there for a few years, and then they started a new division called Silicon Studio, and he became a manager. He traveled back to JPL in Pasadena just to offer me a job. That was pretty flattering to me.

I went to Mountain View for an interview. The way they did interviews, to "hire the best", was to have interviews with each of the members of the team. It seemed okay, but they turned me down. Leo told me that at least one of them said I wouldn't fit into their culture coming from a government agency. Leo hired me anyway. Having failed the interviews, I couldn't be an employee, but I could be a contractor. I went there and lived in an extended stay Motel 6 for a few months, returning home to Los Angeles every week or so. After I became established as part of the team, Leo was able to offer me a job as an employee, and I took it. SGI payed for all the moving expenses for my wife and me, including for selling our house and buying a new one.

CHAPTER 27

1995 - 1998

Silicon Graphics, Inc.

I N FEBRUARY OF 1995, it was kind of a glamorous job. Their work spaces were fantastic. The cubicle walls were purple and there were clouds hanging from the ceiling. Besides making the best 3D graphics machines, SGI also made the best workstations. They used their own version of UNIX called IRIX. They also owned MIPS, the microprocessor chip company. They said there were more MIPS microprocessors in the world than Intel. There were millions of Intel chips in IBM PCs, but MIPS chips were in everything else, like printers. The SGI workstations also had MIPS processors, and they also had higher end processors as well. The MIPS R10000 was the most powerful microprocessor in the world. While I was there, SGI bought Cray Research, and they made a new Cray model based on MIPS R10000 processors. They were rolling in dough.

The Silicon Studio division of SGI was founded to make computer game systems. Our project was called the FireWalker Game Authoring System. In the 6 months I was there, I made the audio players for sampled sound and Midi that worked on both SGI and PC machines, and I made an AVI movie player for the PC with Windows 95. We could also play computer games. The first time I played one, Doom maybe, I began to feel dizzy, headachy, nauseous, and I told someone. He told me I had VR sickness, VR for Virtual Reality. That was new.

The reason I left was that the project failed and I think the whole Silicon Studio went out of business. SGI was really good to its employees. We were all able to transfer to other groups within SGI. This monumental failure was due to what I earlier called the Mythical Man-Month syndrome. Our project was actually three groups of Programmers each with its own manager. Leo was the manager of the group I was in. I don't like criticizing them because the company was really great and the people on the project were really good too. A couple of the Programmers I worked with were famous for things they had done. I had heard of one of them years before I got there.

That was Geoff Brown, creator of the *Deluxe Music Construction Set* for the Amiga computer. I had an Amiga with that program at home, and I was so impressed with it that when I met him I immediately recognized his name. Here I am bragging about all of my technical accomplishments, but I don't think I've ever done anything as great as what Geoff Brown did.

Several years before, when I was still working at JPL in Southern California, my wife was secretary / personal assistant to Dr. Susumu Ohno, a research scientist at the City of Hope Medical Center in Duarte. He was well-known in the field of Genetics. Among his many achievements, he invented a way to turn DNA sequences into music. I don't think it was strictly a mechanical translation. His wife Midori played it on the piano and maybe fixed it up a little bit. After he wrote the score by hand, he gave it to my wife to input into their word processing machine. At that time, there was no Microsoft Word or anything like that. It really was a big machine built just for preparing documents. The large screen was even higher than wide like real documents are.

My wife told me about her assignment, kind of wondering how hard it was going to be with that machine, and I said, Hey, why don't you get an Amiga and use the *Deluxe Music Construction Set?* I had an Amiga with that program and I knew it was good, so I recommended it right away. You can compose music with it and then play it back with the sound of any kind of instrument. She told Dr. Ohno about it and he agreed, so that's what they did. It was a perfect solution to their problem.

Dr. Ohno had his music recorded by professional musicians, and had it performed at a meeting of the Nobel committee in Sweden. He didn't win the Nobel Prize. It's just that he was a very famous scientist and everybody was interested in hearing his music.

MICHAEL DI LORETO

I saw Geoff every day and we worked together a few times, and this is such a cool story that I must have told him about it. I just have no memory of it. Maybe it wasn't really that interesting. To me, though, I'm pleased with my tiny contribution to the work of a famous Scientist and my insignificant connection to a famous Programmer

The problem with Silicon Studio was that they had 15 or 20 really good Programmers all working on the same program. I failed the interview because they thought someone from a big government agency like JPL would work too slowly to be any good. It was just the opposite of what they thought. My best projects at JPL were either a small group of Programmers or just me by myself. Their organization was more top heavy than a government agency and lacked the discipline. Each of those people was probably capable of doing the project themselves, but all of them together could not get anything done. They had even more meetings than in a government office. I was never on a project with three managers at JPL. It was just like when I was with the Data General Systems Division and they started a big project with several new managers and a lot of new Programmers. I said earlier that I thought I could do it myself or with one other person. That's what I thought when I got to SGI. The program just didn't look big enough for 10 people, and they kept hiring more. And just like the manager at Data General who had a copy of the *Mythical Man-Month* on his desk, one of the three managers on the FireWalker project actually told me he knew about the *Mythical Man-Month*, but this project was different. Really.

The way the project was organized, if you asked, "Who is the system designer?", the answer would be nobody or everybody. They had regular design meetings. To start with, design meetings are a really bad sign. Then, everyone was invited. I usually didn't bother. The programming staff had people with a great deal of experience and people with very little. One of the younger guys would work all night. The managers really liked all-nighters. For me, I would come in in the morning and find the system broken. Then I would spend the morning putting it back together.

I don't think I ever worked all night on any project. I just didn't believe in it. I had deadlines that were too short just like everyone else. I think that the more you work through the night, though, the more tired you get, and the more mistakes you make. It's just not worth it.

My father taught me three things. I didn't grow up with him, but when I stayed with him in the Summer of 1968 we talked a little bit. He told me how the UNIVAC Solid State 90 computer didn't have programs in memory. The instructions were layed out on a rotating drum and spaced so that during the time one instruction was executing, the drum would turn to the position of the next instruction. I saw that machine once when I went with him to his office as a child.

The three things were: 1) how to tie a necktie, which I needed to do to go to the UNIVAC classes, and then what I would do every day when I went to work; 2) when you're in the car and waiting to make a left turn, keep the wheels straight ahead, don't turn them left because, if another car hits you from behind, it could push you into oncoming traffic; and 3) there are Programmers who will create a problem with their own program that they won't be able to solve quickly, will work night and day to solve it, and when they finally do, they will be like heroes. If you do your job competently and get your work done without any fuss, you won't get as much attention. I've mentioned the all-nighters at SGI, but I've also seen it happen at JPL. He was right.

MICHAEL DI LORETO

In August of 1996, I transferred to the Alias | wavefront division of SGI. That was a company SGI bought that made 3D graphics tools, or maybe it was two companies, Alias and Wavefront. I worked on the PowerAnimator program. In the 11 months that I was there, I developed a Binary Space Partitioning (BSP) Tree library, plugins for PowerAnimator, and run-time players in OpenGL for IRIX and Direct3D for Windows 95. I also converted the Java maze game to C++, simulating Java 2D graphics with X Library calls.

In July of 1997, I transferred again to the MIPS division of SGI. That was super cool. I joined the group that had made the 3D graphics chip for the Nintendo 64, which was the biggest and best game machine ever. I bought 3 of them, one for myself, which was so good that I bought one for my brother and another one for my sister. I didn't work on the Nintendo 64. When I got there they were already working on a new 3D graphics chip they called Magic Carpet. I verified new 3D graphics hardware, and I developed 3D content conversion, PowerAnimator to Magic Carpet display list format, and a run-time player / demo system on the SGI workstation.

At SGI, I had courses in the MIPS R4000 Computer Architecture and the MIPS R10000 Computer Architecture. The MIPS R4000 was the CPU inside the SGI workstations. While I was there, SGI acquired Cray Research, and they build a new Cray supercomputer based on the MIPS R10000, which they billed as the most powerful microprocessor in the world.

In February of 1998, it seemed like the whole company crashed. They had been working very hard on a new generation super microprocessor and, before they could get it to work, Intel and HP came out with the Itanium processor. It accomplished what SGI / MIPS was trying to do and more. Check my history. I think that's what killed SGI. They had to give up.

Years later I had interviews at Google, two of them some years apart. I didn't apply for a job there. Some recruiters found me and invited me to come for interviews. Google had taken over the Silicon Graphics' campuses in Mountain View. There were two of them. When I started at SGI, I was in a building in the old campus on Shoreline

Blvd. Then they built a new campus across the road and closer to the Shoreline Amphitheater. When I transferred to MIPS, I worked there in a building you may have seen pictures of with a steeply slanting roof. One of my two interviews at Google was in that same building where I had worked before for SGI. That was interesting.

I failed both of my interviews at Google. In the first interview, I sat at a big round table with a whole group of people. They weren't impressed. One of them said something to me about my claiming to be an expert in TCP/IP and then asked me some technical question about it. I didn't know the answer. That's all I remember, except thinking that it would have been better to talk to me about things that I did rather than trying to catch me with hard questions. This brings up another way where maybe I don't think correctly. I never memorize. Technical things, that is. I sometimes do memorize songs and poems in other languages I'm trying to learn.

When I learn something about some software technology, I don't memorize it. I try to understand it. I think that if I understand something, it means I don't have to remember it. I can re-create it. To me, that's what understanding is. I also think I don't have to memorize things because I can look them up. Somewhat contrary to these ideas, but to me complementary, was that I had a really good memory. Without memorizing, I just remembered a lot. And, as I just said, anything I didn't remember I could either re-create or look up.

In my second interview at Google a few years later, I was sitting again at a round table with a group of people. I noticed they were all very young people. I took it they were recent Computer Science graduates who were exceptional in their grades and accomplishments. At some point during the interview, I was talking about debugging, and I said something about guessing what was wrong and then changing something to see if the problem would go away. I don't know if they noticed me saying it in a kind of mocking way as if I thought that anyone would agree with me that that was wrong, but a young lady said, *"That's what I do."* I thought, *"Uh, oh. That's not good."* I was embarrassed. They didn't call me back.

MICHAEL DI LORETO

CHAPTER 28

1998 - 2005

Hewlett-Packard Embedded Software Operation

I WASN'T LAYED OFF from SGI, but I was looking for another job. I found an ad for a job working on a Java Virtual Machine at Hewlett-Packard in Cupertino, and I applied for it. Before I went to my interview, I read a book about Java and did some tutorial exercises. When I got there, I met with individual team members, which, at that point, were only 4 or 5 people altogether. One young lady asked me to write some C code on her white board, a thing you know is really terrible for me to have to do in an interview. I did it, though, and she was really impressed. I didn't think it was that good, just kind of basic stuff, but she enthusiastically said I was "a real coder". In my interview with an older guy who was a manager of a related group, he asked me something about JNI, the Java/Native Interface. It just happened by luck that one of my tutorial exercises was about that, and my answer sounded like I knew something about it. I think it was the only time I ever got hired for a job where I hadn't been recommended by someone.

In February of 1998, I joined the new HP Embedded Software Operation (EMSO) whose project was to make a Java Virtual Machine (JVM) for embedded systems. An embedded system is a computer system inside something you don't generally recognize as a computer, for example, a printer. They are used for controllers, handheld devices, and are often real-time systems.

Sun Microsystems was the creator of the Java language and the Java Virtual Machine. It was okay for HP to develop a Java Virtual Machine as long as they didn't use any Sun code. They called it "clean room" to mean that the software was developed entirely from published specifications. That way they wouldn't be sued. After some long market research process, they settled on ChaiVM for the name of the JVM. The word 'chai' means 'tea' in some languages, and was a play on the word 'java' which is often used to mean 'coffee'. Cute, eh?

Virtual Machine

O'REILLY™

Jon Meyer & Troy Downing

When I got there, they had a C++ implementation of the JVM that was written by some outside group for HP-UX, HP's UNIX-like operating system for their large-scale computer systems. By then, that outside group was gone, and the software was taken over by our small group of four or five Programmers. The manager who hired me was temporary and was soon replaced permanently by Larry Ho. He turned out to be the best manager I ever had.

For workstations, we had PCs with Windows NT. Microsoft Windows was never any good, in my opinion, but Windows NT was actually okay. We used those to connect to the HP-UX system to work on the JVM. My assignment was to make the JVM work on a Brutus Board. I just had to look it up on Google to find out it was really called the BRUTUS SA-1100 Design Verification Platform. This was an evaluation board with a DEC StrongARM microprocessor. It also had a small keyboard and display. There was a C++ cross compiler for StrongARM that ran on the PC.

I compiled the JVM on the PC and downloaded it into the Brutus Board on my desk. The real-time operating system we used was called VxWorks. This was the first embedded ChaiVM.

This, of course, didn't just work. It's often a big job to port a C++ program from one platform to another. The JVM does many machine dependent things making it harder. Naturally, I learned the ARM Assembler Language right away. I was very impressed. The elegance of the ARM instruction set reminded me of the Data General NOVA, but it was much more powerful.

The real difficulty, though, was the JVM program itself. It was a very big C++ program, and it was just very badly written. The developers were gone, so I never met them, but I had the impression it was their first C++ program and they wanted to use every possible feature. You have to know C++ to understand what I mean. C++ has so many things in it that seem very advanced, and that can lead new Programmers to do really bad things. First of all, a good program, no matter how big it is, has to be simple. Remember what I said? *"If you don't understand it, you can't make it work."* Unfortunately, C++ promotes coding that can be almost impossible to understand. As good an idea as Object-Oriented Programming may be, it's really prone to abuse. I think I already said something about operator overloading and constructors. C++ also has multiple inheritance, and so many other dangerous features that, even if you wanted to, you could never use them all.

To me, one of the best things about the design of Java, which is also Object-Oriented, was that they left out things like multiple inheritance and operator overloading. The other excellent thing they did at Sun was to keep the design of the language to themselves. There are not academics all over the world making up new features like there are for C++.

On my own, since I had a PC on my desk, I ported the JVM to run on Windows NT. Someone complained that that was not what our project was supposed to do, but just about as soon as it was working everyone stopped using the HP-UX version.

I ported ChaiVM to Windows CE for 3 different processors: ARM, Hitachi SH3, and MIPS. ChaiVM was the first JVM certified by Microsoft for the Pocket PC. I did the certification process myself. I became the VM Technology Lead for the HP Embedded Software Operation (EMSO). Then we moved to HP Headquarters in Palo Alto, and I worked there for some time.

HP had a calculator division in Melbourne, Australia that was making a Java PDA they called Calypso. I made a Linux version of ChaiVM and I traveled to Melbourne to help them with integration and troubleshooting.

There was an Open Group Research Institute in Grenoble, France who was developing the TurboChai Ahead-Of-Time compiler. When I worked with them they had changed their name to Silicomp. I developed the run-time support, and did integration, debugging and porting to multiple platforms. I traveled to Grenoble twice for this project.

Siemens AG in Fürth, Germany made a real-time process control system that they wanted to program in Java. I provided them with a model for fast interrupt handling in Java for ChaiVM on their own real-time operating system, RMOS. Java does not have any interrupt handling capability. I invented it just for the Siemens project. I traveled to Germany to help them with it.

I developed the Java support for HP Jornada PDAs that were made by a division of HP in Singapore. Too bad I didn't get to go there. I created the ActiveX control for Java applets running in the Internet Explorer on Jornadas. ChaiVM was then bundled with Jornadas, either in ROM or on an accompanying CD.

After working on the big Object-Oriented JVM for awhile, and endlessly debugging it, I had the idea that it really should be much simpler. So, as an experiment, I wrote my own JVM in C by following the SUN specifications in the great book, the JAVA Virtual Machine. I say the book was great because it clearly explains everything you need to know to write a JVM.

Another group was established to make a smaller, faster JVM they called MicroChaiVM. By coincidence, my smaller, faster JVM was already working, so instead of starting a whole project to create one, they just used mine. MicroChaiVM was an independent implementation of CLDC and MIDP, so they did have a real development project. But I wasn't part of it. They were able to use my JVM without any trouble, and didn't need my help.

Java does memory management by a technique called Garbage Collection. This is kind of a big deal and there are books written about it. The idea is that the JVM keeps track of Java Objects in memory and, when one is no longer in use, the memory is freed or deallocated. Our particular Garbage Collection method was called Mark-And-Sweep. Essentially, objects in use are marked, and the rest are swept away.

Naturally, my own JVM had a small, fast garbage collector, but it didn't work by mark-and-sweep. It used reference counting. There's supposed to be something wrong with that, some fatal flaw. I just don't remember what it was. I think the difference might be something like washing your dishes every time you eat versus washing them all once at the end of the week. Which one is more efficient? Well, since my JVM was just a play program, it was okay to try a different technique just to see how it might be done.

At some point, the performance of ChaiVM became a big issue. Some customer acceptance depended on much better benchmark test results. Two of us were then charged with building a faster Garbage Collector for ChaiVM, with a very short deadline to achieve specific performance the customer was demanding. I couldn't just lift my personal one because it didn't work the same way at all. It was necessary to write a new one. My co-worker, Xiaoyi Guo, and I worked all day every day for it must have been a couple of weeks to replace the Garbage Collector in ChaiVM. We got it done and achieved the desired results and everyone was happy.

Xiaoyi and I worked so well together that to me it was a perfect example of Pair Programming, something I would read about some time later. I have a book about that, and another one about Extreme Programming. I'm generally down on books about software development methodology because to me they're just not realistic. The writer of Extreme Programming said that their ideas came from watching what real Programmers do. That seemed unique to me because the other methodologies all seemed to be from the point of view of managers or academics and, even when imposed on a project, Programmers generally ignore them as best we can in order to do what needs to be done. Not only don't they want to know what Programmers really do, the ultimate goal of some of the methodologies is to eliminate Programmers altogether.

I had several experiences with software development methodologies at JPL, which was at an earlier time in my chronology. I've talked before about how they wanted documentation and lines-of-code counts. Sometimes the documentation was in the form of a "Design Language". A design language is supposed to be used to create a design before writing a program. The problem for me is that the design languages are not executable by a computer. Design languages are similar to programming languages, but they don't work.

Programmers hate documentation. Managers always want it, but Programmers don't want to do it. It's really a pain when near the end of a project the software has to be documented. That involves long hours of wasted time producing totally useless documents. One project I worked on mandated that all software be documented in something called Crisp PDL, a design language very similar to a programming language. Someone there had the great idea to write a program to convert PL/M code to Crisp PDL. I think it was mainly just reformatting the code. They did that and put the "documentation" in binders on shelves, and everyone was happy. The Managers had their documents and the Programmers didn't have to do anything.

Garbage Collection

Algorithms for Automatic Dynamic Memory Management

Richard Jones
Rafael Lins

I designed and implemented a new Just-In-Time (JIT) compiler with code generators for Intel X86 on Windows NT and Linux, and ARM on Windows CE. It was then integrated into MicroChaiVM. I completed two patent applications for my inventions that were part of the JIT. One of them was for what was called "A Multi-Module Interpreter", which I can't explain right now, but I think was a design for an interpreter that worked on two levels. I just downloaded a copy of the patent application, but it was written by some patent attorney and I can't make any sense of it. I don't even know why it's called "multi-module". I think the attorney made that up.

The two levels had to do with the way control was transferred from the interpreter to compiled code and back. That involved a continuation technique rather than recursive calls which I thought was an innovation. That patent application is funny. In the middle of several pages of gibberish there's a diagram that consists of two boxes, one above the other, with a bi-directional arrow connecting the two. The top box is labeled "Upper Level Module" and the bottom box is the "Lower Level Module". I guess that explains it.

The other patent was for "Converting Byte Code Instructions To A New Instruction Set". I designed a new generic instruction set that was intermediate between Java byte code and real machine instructions. Java byte code is very compact and is not a very good representation from which to generate machine code. So, instead of generating machine instructions directly from the byte code, I converted the byte code to my new representation, and then generated the machine code from that. That's two steps instead of one, and looks like the long way around again. However, after the first step, the second step was much easier. It still seems like too much work, doesn't it? But notice I was generating machine code for two different microprocessors. The first step was the same for both, of course, but the second step had to be different, so simplifying that made targeting a second CPU that much easier and faster to implement. Do you believe it now?

I provided ChaiVM for HP-UX, Linux and Windows 2000/XP to the HP OpenView project in Roseville, where it was used as an embedded component in the OpenView Operations for Windows

(OVOW) product. I added 64-bit support to ChaiVM for Itanium (IA64) processors running HP-UX and Linux.

The Embedded Software Operation (EMSO) was a startup business inside of HP. It had five years to come up with products that would sell and make money. When that didn't happen, the business was shut down. The only real users of ChaiVM were the HP Imaging and Printing Group (IPG) who put it in LaserJet printers.

I was then transferred to the HP Imaging and Printing Group (IPG) where I provided ChaiVM on LynxOS with MIPS and Coldfire processors for Embedded Web Services. Java was not used at all for printing, but by using Java, printers could serve web pages.

CHAPTER 29

2005 - 2007

Hewlett-Packard Enterprise Systems

I N MARCH OF 2005, I transferred to the Enterprise Systems Java Section of HP. When EMSO shut down, Larry Ho, who was my manager there, transferred to that organization, while I went to the Printing Group. As the manager of Enterprise Systems Java, he hired me. I'm kind of proud of that, that a manager I worked for before thinks highly enough of me to want to hire me again. And I wasn't out of work. He actually came to me to offer me the job.

I became part of the Enterprise Systems Core Java Team. Enterprise systems, in case it's not obvious, are HP's large-scale computers. The older ones were built on the PA-RISC architecture, and the newer ones were Itanium (IA64). Our team in Cupertino was only 5 people, with several more in Bangalore, India. Our job was to port Sun's JVM to HP-UX and to fix bugs and make improvements to the JVM for HP-UX. Sun owns the JVM, of course, but they made a deal with HP to allow us to use their code. It was an ongoing project for us because whenever Sun came out with a new version of the JVM, we had to port it again.

Mostly what I did was fix bugs or review bug fixes. They had a good system for reporting and tracking bugs, and a rule that whenever a bug was fixed it was reviewed by someone else. It was a good system, very efficient. HP had three levels of customer support. The lowest level just basically fielded customers' problems, made sure their license was okay, and so on. The next level could solve general problems. The highest level could deal with real Java problems. They were either able to help the Customer directly or they could submit a bug to the JVM. Then the bug would come to our group to fix. Bugs were submitted internally too.

HP's biggest computer was called the SuperDome. I never saw one, so I don't know if it looked like a dome. It was a huge multiprocessor system, with up to 256 Itanium processors.

Performance was always a really big deal for HP. The people working on the operating system and the people working on the JVM were always trying to improve performance. For a multiprocessor system, performance is expected to scale up. That is, a program should run faster when it has more processors. Most programs don't scale up because they are serial in nature. To scale up, a program has to be written for parallel processing. To test that, HP had a Java benchmark program that had as many parallel processes as there were processors. Ideally, a graph of the performance should show a straight line that goes up with the number of processors. The main reason a parallel program may not speed up linearly is that the parallel processes are not entirely independent. If any one of them ever has to wait for something from another one, that makes it less parallel, and you get less speed-up. In real programs, there's always something like that because the different processes inevitably have to share something in order to be useful. The test that had many parallel processes that didn't interact with each other at all was artificially contrived just to test for ideal performance speed-up.

The Java parallel processing performance benchmark was working as expected, getting the linear speed-up it was supposed to get. Then a new version of Java came out where the program did not speed up with more processors. That was submitted as a bug to the JVM. Somebody was assigned to it before I got there, and they worked on it, but didn't find out what was wrong. But since it was just an artificial benchmark test, the bug had low priority.

In the Java Section, they had a process of aging bugs. That is, a regular report was produced for the Section manager that had statistics about the number of bugs and the time taken to resolve them. They wanted the average time to resolve a bug to be as short as possible.

Normally, bugs were fixed pretty quickly, so there wasn't a problem, except that when that one performance bug was outstanding for more than a year, it was messing up the average, and annoying the Section Manager. I guess he probably had to report the team's performance to higher managers.

Someone new was assigned to that bug, but he didn't do anything. I never know if it's because I'm the best one to solve the problem, or if the other guy is busy and the bug is not that important, but for whatever reason, they assigned it to me.

It really was a very difficult bug. I ran tests to try to see what might be wrong, but there was no obvious failure. Fortunately, I was able to solve it, but it totally depended on all my previous experience not just with debugging in general, but also with working on multiprocessor systems on the TimeWarp project at JPL. I already knew generally, what many people know, that the main obstacle to multiprocessor performance is bottlenecks. That is, as I said, something that causes the parallel processes to wait for something. I only meant to say that I already knew that and that I didn't have to learn it for that bug.

One of the machines I ported TimeWarp to was the BBN Butterfly multiprocessor. The machine I worked on had 84 68020 processors in a shared memory configuration. The reason the machine was called the "Butterfly" was that a diagram of the way all the processors were connected to each other looked like a butterfly. That interconnection topology was called an Omega Network.

I said the memory was shared, but it was not like there was one big memory that all the processors could access. Each processor had its own 4M of memory, but could access the memory in all the other processor nodes by memory address. It was as if there was one big memory, but when a CPU tried to access memory, hardware would decide whether it was a local address or not. If the address was local, the CPU accessed its own memory normally. If the address was not local, the hardware would determine which node in the network had the address, and then make a request through the network to that other processor node to access the memory there. The BBN Butterfly had distributed memory like the HyperCube, but accessed it at the memory address level. The

HyperCube could not access the memory in other nodes at all. The software had to send messages from node to node. A funny thing I did to port TimeWarp to the Butterfly was to create a message passing system using the shared memory to communicate between the nodes. I spent about a week in Boston at the BBN Headquarters doing that.

So, before I started on that performance bug, I was already an expert in distributed multiprocessor systems, both with shared memory and without. The HP SuperDome is a large distributed multiprocessor system with shared memory. The interconnection network on the SuperDome was not physically like the BBN Butterfly's, but otherwise the setup was very similar. Each processor node had its own local memory, but the system made it look like all the memory on all the nodes was one big memory, and access to it was at the memory address level.

I also knew before I started that access to local memory is very fast, and access to remote memory is much slower. Imagine that. And another thing about accessing memory remotely is that the node that receives the memory request can only service one request at a time. It's very fast, but if, for example, several nodes all request memory from the same node at the same time, there's going to be a slight delay. In normal operation, that's not bothersome. But now imagine that 255 of the 256 processors repeatedly ask the same 1 processor for memory, and it shouldn't be hard to see that the whole system is behaving serially. It's the worst case bottleneck.

I considered whether there were other possible causes of the performance problem, but as soon as I learned that the SuperDome was a distributed shared memory system, I knew what I was looking for, something like excessive reliance on some particular area of shared memory. The hard part was going to be how to prove that, and how to pin down what code was doing it and why. Another question was why this just happened in the newer version of the JVM and not the older one, which still continued to work the way it was supposed to.

I needed more information. I found a guy in the HP-UX group who had a cubicle on the same floor where mine was, and I went and talked to him. It turned out he had a tool that could map out section by section where all the memory in the program was located on the processor nodes. He had to fix it up a little for me to use, then he gave it to me. I think that tool might have needed some special privilege to run it, but he also arranged that for me. I don't remember all that that tool did, but it may have also had some helpful usage statistics.

It was painstaking work analyzing all the memory sections in that very large program, the Java Virtual Machine, looking at them from the operating system point of view, and matching them to a listing of the program's sections from building it. In fact, I was able to pin it down to a section of memory in the JVM that was used by all the processors all the time. I was therefore able to explain why the performance test didn't speed up. Next I had to explain why that didn't happen in the previous version of the JVM. I had to do the same kind of analysis again, and I found out that, for no obvious reason, Sun had rearranged the memory sections in the new version in a way that caused the problem that did not happen with the old arrangement.

The problem was solved. I wrote a report explaining what I found and distributed it to my manager and to the rest of the Java Section. Obviously, it took a lot of explaining, a lot more than I did just now. Everyone was happy, right? Nope. They didn't believe it. I was still pretty much a newcomer, and some of the people had been there for a long time and were more qualified than I was. My manager, Larry Ho, asked me to write another report explaining the problem more. I did that and gradually the more senior people started coming around. There really was a lot more to it than I just talked about here, and it really was very difficult to explain. But I was right.

HP had a thing they called an e-award. It was like a gift certificate for some outstanding achievement that an employee got by email, thus the 'e' in the "e-award". I think it was $100 for solving a problem that none of the more senior people could solve for more than a year. Thanks.

I was also a member of the Java Customer Satisfaction Team. This was a very small group, I think there were just 3 of us and the manager. The Java Section's top Java guru was in that team. When a big customer had a big problem, it would come to that team. It didn't have to be a JVM bug like we dealt with in the Core JVM team. It could be a problem with someone's application or how to do something that was technically difficult. I liked doing that because I was always good at working with customers directly to help them with whatever they needed. It was a good position for me. I was the only one who was in both Core JVM and Customer Satisfaction at the same time. I was the only one who could submit a bug from a customer and then work on the bug.

In China, there was a big HP installation at some tax agency. There were 3 large HP servers in a cluster arrangement, meaning they were connected to each other to distribute web service requests. Their project had been in development for some time and was soon to go live.

But there was a problem. They used a PC to generate transactions to test the system, and the system was failing intermittently. This had been going on for a long time. About a year earlier, they asked for help from Java Customer Satisfaction, and the guy I mentioned as HP's top Java guru got the problem. He didn't know what was wrong, so he submitted a bug to the operating system. The HP-UX group didn't have enough information to do anything, so the bug just sat. Now that the Chinese Tax Bureau was planning to go live soon, this problem suddenly became urgent.

The Chinese were demanding that this problem be solved. Their system was in a place that was not connected to the Internet, so they wanted people to go there. And they wanted everybody, not just for Java, but also the operating system, database management system, and web service software providers. All these people were supposed to go to China to solve this big problem. The salesman was saying this was extremely important because it could lead to $50,000,000 in business.

Instead, they assigned the problem to me. Sound familiar? But I didn't get to go to China. HP did a really good thing by setting up the same configuration of 3 HP servers in a cluster with a PC to send transactions all in their Beijing office. They could run the same test and reproduce the failure. They assigned a person there to help me to make sure I could connect to the servers and the PC and run the test myself from my cubicle in Cupertino. Because of the time difference,

I shifted my schedule to work later in the evening to be able to talk to my colleague there.

It was a pretty hard problem. It was also about Christmas time and holidays were slowing things down. I think I worked on it for a few weeks altogether. I located the bug in the BEA Web Services software. I didn't have their code, but I had a tool called JAD that could decompile Java byte code into Java source code. I found they were using an operating system service that turned out to be slightly different on HP-UX than on Sun's operating system SunOS, and the way they were doing it was causing a timing problem, that is, an intermittent failure.

I found out that BEA had an office in Beijing, and I contacted someone there who worked on the WebLogic Server software. I told him about the problem, and I asked him to make a change to their code to fix it. I told him what code to change and how to change it. He did that and sent a new version to my colleague at HP in Beijing. She installed the software and ran the test. It worked. Problem solved. I think it was the best compliment I've ever had when someone I never saw, but who clearly understood the magnitude of the issue, told me, *"That was a wonderful thing you did!"*

But it wasn't done yet. The BEA manager in Cupertino objected to changing their code, insisting that it was an HP-UX problem and HP should fix it. We had a meeting with the BEA manager, my manager, other HP people, and the BEA software group on the phone from Bangalore. I explained what happened, and the BEA manager argued, but the lead BEA software guy in India said *"It's just one line of code, it makes it more portable, no problem."* or something like that.

Now the problem really was solved. And I got another e-award, this time $125. This bigger amount was no doubt due to my saving HP $50,000,000 of business. Well, probably not. But I really did do a good job, and at least one person in China really did appreciate it.

That situation is a good example of going to where the problem is wherever it is. Some big problems are like that. No one had any idea where the problem could be. That's why the Chinese tax bureau wanted people representing every part of the system to all go to their place to work on it. It could have been the operating system, the Java virtual machine, the database management system, or the web services software. Often it's more likely to be in the application, but then what part of the application? I just skipped to the end saying where the bug turned out to be, but a lot went into how I got there. I didn't just disassemble all the Java code hoping to find something wrong. I was looking at that code because my investigation led me there.

I've said how the normal first step to solving a software problem is to reproduce the failure. I think most Programmers know that. The way you do that is to run the program again in order to see the failure again. If the failure repeats, the next step is to try to catch it in the debugger or by adding print statements. If it doesn't repeat, the usual approach is the one-step guessing technique. Most of the time, though, the Programmer has the source code, so there's a way to find out what's wrong by changing things to see what happens. If they don't have the code, they're stuck.

Another difficulty with this particular failure was that nobody knew what part of the overall system was failing. People working on the different parts had no reason to think the failure was in their part, so they didn't look. I mentioned how the Java guru sent the bug to the HP-UX group.

With my knowledge and experience, I was able to work on every part of the system. My role at that time was working on the Java Virtual Machine, but I was just as much of an expert in operating systems, programming languages, database management systems, communications, device drivers, as well as applications. There are Systems Programmers who never work on applications. I could see the whole system from every point of view.

As I was saying, the usual way of working on a bug is to reproduce the problem by running the program again, seeing it fail again, and then changing the program to find out more. That works for most of the people most of the time. In this case, I could run the test and repeat the failure, but I couldn't change anything and, even if I could, it was unknown what code to change.

My approach then was to write my own program that did the same thing as the system that failed to see if I could make it fail the same

MICHAEL DI LORETO

way. If I could do that, I would then be able to do experiments to see why it failed and how to fix it. So, I had to do the same thing the web services software did, and do it the same way. That involved using an operating system service that had to do with getting a notification of an arriving message. I mentioned how solving this problem took a few weeks. This is what I was doing.

When I successfully reproduced the failure with my own program on our own HP-UX system in Cupertino, and I could reliably make the failure repeat, I fixed it. Naturally, to test my program that simulated the web services software, I also had to write my own program to send it transactions. Those two things were necessary to replicate the system in China with a PC for sending transactions to an HP-UX cluster of servers. See how writing one program often involves writing another one?

Now, the web services code that had the bug was code that was portable across operating systems because it was written in Java. It was used a lot on Sun systems without ever having a problem like this. That's why BEA was so sure it wasn't their code that was at fault. To deal with that, I got access to a Sun machine in our building, and tested my program there. With my code in the state before I fixed it, it never failed on the Sun. Of course, my job there was on HP-UX, but I was also a long-time expert in Sun systems, so I could work on both systems equally well.

Many operating system services are portable from one system to another, but this time the system service had some fairly small, but critically important difference. It took some very careful study to learn the details of that system service, what was different between the two operating systems, why it failed on one but not the other, and how to fix it so that it would be portable, not having different code for different systems. When I told the BEA guy in Beijing what code to change and how to change it, it was not an experiment or a guess. I'd already spent many hours proving exactly what was wrong and exactly how to make it right.

I wrote this part intending to explain how some really complex problem can be solved in a systematic way. I'm afraid, though, that it might just sound like bragging, and I realize that, as a lesson in programming, it may not help much to say that you have to start out already knowing everything. Presumably, if I weren't there, someone would have eventually solved it somehow. All I can say is that if you're working on tough problems, the more you know the better. Along with that, I would add that learning things is something very important for a Programmer to do.

At HP, I had courses in HP-UX Internals and IA64 Linux Internals. Sometime previously I had had courses in Sun Microsystems SunOS (Solaris) Internals and DEC VAX VMS Internals. I've already mentioned courses in UNIVAC 1108 EXEC 8 Internals and IBM 360 OS Internals. I also had a course in RedHat Linux Device Drivers.

CHAPTER 30

2007 - 2009

Hewlett-Packard Atalla
Security Products

I N JUNE OF 2007, HP was cutting costs in the Enterprise
Organization. Nobody was layed off, but they offered people
generous early retirement plans. Many people took them. I might have
too but I don't think I was close enough to retirement yet. For the people
who were staying at HP, they held a job fair where several groups who
needed people presented their opportunities. I was impressed by a group
called HP Atalla Security Products, and I managed to transfer there.

The Atalla group was a separate business inside of HP. It was a
company HP acquired that was named for its founder, Mohamed
Martin Atalla. I read that he was the inventor of the PIN for ATMs in
1972 and a machine called the "Atalla Box" for secure verification of the
PINs. The group at HP continued the development and marketing of
that machine as well as other security products. We were in a separate
facility inside HP in Cupertino where we had a different badge to get
in and where we were cut off from the outside network.

The purpose of the device was to verify PINs from ATMs at banks.
The PIN is encrypted at the ATM and sent to a server that in turn hands
it over to the device for verification. The device has a master key inside
that can verify the PIN without decrypting it. The unencrypted PIN
does not exist anywhere, not in the device, and not on the server or in
the customer's records. The device is enclosed in a box that if opened

causes the master key, which also does not exist anywhere else, to be destroyed. Their motto was to not trust anyone, not even the IT person.

I worked on something called the Secure Key Manager (SKM). This was software on a server than managed encryption keys. It turns out that organizations have many keys. The keys are all encrypted and stored in a database. There are keys for decrypting not only data, but also other keys in a hierarchy of keys. I maintained the Client libraries in C, C++ and Java for Windows, Linux and HP-UX, and I supported development partners. I ported the SKM Server software including the Linux Kernel and Device Drivers to the HP ProLiant ML115 G5 platform.

I developed board test and setup applications in C# using Microsoft Visual Studio for the Secure Print Module (SPM) manufacturing process and end-user tools. I helped debug the networking code in the SPM Loader, which runs without an OS on the PowerPC single-board computer. I developed the SPM Cryptographic Test Personality, which was an application program that ran on the Integrity RTOS.

I reviewed code and did some programming for the PIC microcontroller, and I reviewed formal specifications written in the Z language and contributed one axion. On my own, just to see if I could do it, I implemented the AES encryption algorithm from the published specification, and my program passed the official test that comes with the standard.

In February of 2009, the Atalla group was downsizing, and I was selected to be laid off. I wasn't just thrown out, though. HP was a great company to work for. They gave me plenty of time to find another job within HP with full access and full pay. To help me out, two people in Atalla wrote letters of recommendation for me. One of them was Steven Wierenga, an HP Distinguished Technologist, and the other was Jane Blanchard, my manager. The letters worked, I was able to transfer to another group in Cupertino. These two letters are so flattering that I hung onto them, and I'm including them here. They both obviously wanted to help me, but I insist that everything they said was true without exaggeration. I promise I did not change a word.

I'm chief technologist in the Atalla Security Products group (in Cupertino, 46L). I'm technical leader for our Secure Advantage Enterprise Key Management strategy and products. I've gotten to know Michael Di Loreto and his abilities over the past year from his work on two recent projects: the Secure Key Manager (SKM) Client SDK, and the SKM SE Server.

Our organization was notified of a 50% budget cut and WFR last Monday, due to sudden decommitment of funding from other divisions. As you might expect, any cut this large must impact top developers as well as ordinary. When I found Michael was included, I immediately went to him to say how much I appreciate his great work, what a loss it was to our team, and offer to be a reference for any opportunities he found, whether HP or external.

Our SKM Client SDK is based on C and Java (JCE) client side source code libraries licensed from a technology partner in April 2008. Michael was our only developer assigned. From a cold start, in a matter of weeks he put all the licensed source code, test cases, and documentation under source control system; got all build and target environments running; built, debugged, and fixed broken and incomplete test programs; helped create regular build and QA processes, and began implementing HP-defined modifications and extensions. He also identified and reconciled differences between the C and JCE libraries, and verified object builds/installs for our 3 reference target platforms (Windows, Linux, HP-UX), so a total of 6 different build and runtime/test environments. Michael also produced and the final SDK package on CD ROM, including several custom SDK packages for HP external partners. Michael has also been providing developer support for our HP and external SDK users. All these details don't matter much, except to show that Michael is a very quick learner, very self-sufficient (but a great team member), very productive, very thorough, and quickly solves any problem he finds or is handed to him.

Our SKM SE Server project included Michael and another engineer porting our released SKM 1.1 Server code (DL360

G5, CentOS Linux) to a different and unknown hardware platform (the ML115 G5), on a very fast schedule, working at partner facilities in Redwood City, using the partner's development environment. We had a 6 weeks late start due to contract issues, but when Michael was finally assigned and gained source code access, he jumped right in, learned whatever he needed quickly, discovered and debugged the necessary drivers and changes, ran all applicable functional and performance tests, and delivered fully functional object code to our QA team. Making up for all of the 6 weeks late start!

What makes Michael exceptional to me is his versatility, quick learning ability, eagerness to try new things, and dependability. If he is interested in your project, without hesitation I recommend that you grab him. Please feel free to call or email me for further discussion.

Best Regards
Steven Wierenga
HP Distinguished Technologist

-----Original Message-----
From: Blanchard, Jane
Sent: Tuesday, January 13, 2009 1:58 PM
To: Xiao, Xiaomao
Subject: Strong recommendation for Michael Di Loreto

Xiaomao,

Michael is one of the best engineer I have ever worked with.

Last year I took on a program for key management product. It required 3rd party vendor to port their server code on new platform. They estimate 8 weeks of time and can not come up with the resource to do it. I send Michael to vendor's location to work on it. Two weeks, he brought server code up on the new platform. Michael has no prior knowledge about the

server code, or the new platform. More impressive is
Michael created the porting document and he become
expert in this area. My vendor is asking advice from
him now.

Michael is not ordinary internal transfers. His speed
impress a lot folks here. It is unfortunate the
program is cancelled and the engineers who worked on
the program no longer have job. I really hope HP can
keep him, because he is that good.

BTW, I was working on recommend him to be promoted
to Master. I am a big fan of him. :-)

Thanks,

Jane Blanchard
Program Manager
Hewlett-Packard
Atalla Security Products
19091 Pruneridge Ave., MS 4441
Cupertino, CA 95014
Tel: (408) 447-2168
Fax: (408) 447-5525
email: jane.blanchard@hp.com
web: www.atalla.com

Steve and Jane didn't mention it, but the project was supposed to
be led by the top software guy in the group with me assisting him. But
something happened to him, he got sick or something, so I had to do
the project by myself. As seems to often be the case, I went to a big
office that had the computers and things in it, but no people. As usual,
I was all alone there all day every day. There was no one to talk to and
I figured everything out on my own. That guy that was supposed to
do the project was very good, he really was the top Programmer, but
I think my doing the job alone was probably faster and more efficient
than the two of us working together.

CHAPTER 31

2009 - 2010

Hewlett-Packard Emerging
Platform Group

IN FEBRUARY OF 2009, I transferred to the HP Emerging Platform Group. The Xiaomao to whom Jane addressed her letter for me was the manager who hired me. The project there was to build an Android tablet, something like an iPad, but a little before the iPad came out. The group was doing Google Android Platform Development for the Compaq Airlife 100 netbook. I mainly worked on the Volume Daemon and Mount Service to extend the SD Card functionality to multiple devices. I did general debugging in C, C++ and Java on Linux and Windows.

A *Superprogrammer* does every programming chore faster and better than most other Programmers. I considered both Steen Brydum and Martin Orton to be Superprogrammers. They were both a little older than me and had begun programming earlier. They were technically more advanced and had greater accomplishments than me. Steen Brydum was the visionary leader of Management Applied Programming who I followed when I worked there two different times. Martin Orton was renowned at JPL before I got there. His reputation was so great that it seemed like everyone knew and respected him. I'm proud to have been associated with both of them.

I brought this up here as a way of explaining something I routinely did that I think was unusual, but that I think is relevant to my programming lessons. I've mentioned before that my rule of thumb when planning a program was to always plan on writing three more. I said that was to do things like generate test data, to facilitate testing, and to analyze test results. Another thing that's like that was to write programs to do experiments whose purpose was to learn how some unfamiliar technology worked before incorporating it into the real program. That's not the same thing as play programs like the CPU simulators I wrote that were just learning exercises and not specifically for any real project. Still another kind of program that I often wrote were little tools for me to use in doing my work. Programmers have to do a lot of little odd jobs aside from the programming they're assigned to do. Many of those things can be done by hand. But I claim it as a Superprogrammer technique to write programs to do those odd jobs. For one thing, I think that it's an advanced skill to be able to conceive and write programs so quickly and reliably that small, even one-time, chores can be done faster than doing them by hand. For another thing, why do things by hand when you have a computer? Another of my sayings: "*Let the computer do the work.*"

It's hard to think of examples of this kind of program. They're just not memorable. I would often use C for programs like that, but sometimes I would use Perl because of some library module or other than was not readily available in C. On this Android project, I had some reason to want to download a file from a web site, and I chose Python to do it because of its library. I think it was just a play program to learn Python, but I also think it was related to what I was doing. The reason I remember it at all is that a co-worker sitting across from me was having a problem. He was doing something that needed to be done right away and he was under some pressure. But he needed to download a file from a web site and, for some reason, the download was failing using the browser. In frustration, he said something to me about it, and I said I had a program that might be able to do that. I gave it to him and it worked. To me, something that makes a program really good and memorable is if it helps someone to do something they want to do.

I was there for about a year and a half when two things happened. First of all, the Apple iPad was far better than anything we were trying to build. Then HP acquired Palm, a company that made smart phones. That ended our project, as well as the bigger HP group that was making HP's own smart phone. I was about to be laid off again, but again HP gave me the opportunity to transfer to another group.

MICHAEL DI LORETO

CHAPTER 32

2010 - 2011

Hewlett-Packard Palm

IN JULY OF 2010, I joined HP Palm. The Palm machines ran Palm's own operating system, WebOs, and all the applications were written in JavaScript. Based on my prior JVM experience, I was assigned to work on the Google V8 JavaScript Virtual Machine. Besides that, I also created JS Heap Analysis and Code Coverage tools. I programmed in C++ and JavaScript on Linux for WebOs targets. I was one of only two people working on the JavaScript Virtual Machine.

In April of 2011, I left HP for good. With 13 years there, I became an official HP retiree. I have a little badge that says so. The reason I left was that my manager from the HP Enterprise Java group, Larry Ho, who was then working for Oracle, offered me a job. This would be the third time he was my manager. The first time I was already there in the ChaiVM group when he joined it as the manager, and the second and third time he was the manager who hired me. I've said before what a good thing I think it was that managers who knew me would hire me again.

CHAPTER 33

2011 - 2017

Oracle Corporation

I BECAME A CONTRIBUTING Member of the Technical Staff for Oracle Corporation at their headquarters in Redwood Shores. If you've ever driven by there on the 101, you can see it from the freeway, its several tall green buildings looking like the Emerald City of Oz. It was really cool. My title was Oracle's highest technical position, equivalent to Director on the management side.

The group I joined did QA for Oracle's JDeveloper product. That was a graphical user interface tool for developing Java applications for mobile devices. Applications created with JDeveloper were portable to both iOS (iPhone and iPad) and Android phones and tablets. To test JDeveloper, I used it to create native mobile applications on MacOS. I developed web applications using JDeveloper and Java on Windows and Linux. I was a part-time developer of the MonkeyTalk test automation system for the Oracle Mobile Applications Framework (MAF) using Java, JavaScript and Objective-C.

At Oracle, I had courses in BEA WebLogic Server 9.0 System Administration, Oracle 9i Database Performance Tuning and something called NetObjectives Design Patterns Explained.

In about August of 2017, I accepted a voluntary severance from Oracle, which was the same thing as being layed off, but with a good severance package. I don't know exactly why that happened. By then, I had moved to Las Vegas and was a remote worker. Larry Ho had left Oracle, and I had a different manager. He never said anything, but I generally observe that managers like to get their groups together for meetings and they like their people to be there in person. I was also probably twice as old as everyone else, almost 67, and nobody ever said anything about that either, but I've also noticed that some managers like younger workers who are easier to control. Of course, my speculations may not be right at all. The manager could very well have had some other reason to get rid of me. Too bad. I thought if I could work one more year, I would have an even 50 years of professional experience. As it is, 49 years doesn't sound nearly as good, does it? Oh, well.

CHAPTER 34

Conferences and Associations

I ATTENDED IJCAI CONFERENCES (International Joint Conference on Artificial Intelligence) in Karlsruhe, Germany (1983), UCLA (1985), Chambery, France (1993), and Montreal, Canada (1995).

I attended COLING conferences (International Conference on Computational Linguistics) at Stanford University (1984), and Budapest, Hungary (1988). I had a week-long tutorial course in Prolog programming at Stanford using their DEC PDP/10 computer. Prolog was a language designed for Natural Language Processing (NLP). Recursive definitions of grammatical structures could be coded and interpreted in a way similar to formal grammars.

I was a member of the Digital Computer Association (DCA) which they claimed to be the world's oldest computer society. There weren't any meetings or newsletters, just an annual banquet in a big ballroom somewhere in Los Angeles. I attended two of them with my wife, where we sat at a big round table with people I didn't know. Their thing was to save wine bottle corks all year and then toss them at people at the other tables. It was all for fun, but there were computer pioneers there. I remember seeing Grace Hopper, the inventor of Cobol, recognizable in her Navy uniform.

There was a big screen in the front of the room to project slides for presentations. I remember one in particular where there was the usual scientific-looking pie chart with a caption that said, *"90% of everything is stupid."* I thought that was great.

I regularly attended the Los Angeles Chapter of the ACM monthly meetings. They were held in a small ballroom in a restaurant. There were always very interesting presentations. I saw John Backus there one time, the famous inventor of Fortran. I met him in the elevator. He gave a talk about Red languages, where "red" was short for "reduction". I ordered his book from IBM, and I must still have it here somewhere. I also saw Peter Naur there a different time. I don't remember his talk, but Backus and Naur together invented the Backus-Naur Form (BNF).

At another meeting, the presenter was talking about the perceived danger of computers becoming too smart. He likened it to the Frankenstein story where the creation turns on the creator. Everyone remembers HAL 9000 in *2001: A Space Odyssey*. The point I remember was that he said approximately, "*The most powerful computer in the world couldn't outwit a goldfish.*" That fear never went away, though. Now people think Artificial Intelligence (AI) will soon destroy the world, or at least all the humans in it. I just saw someone on TV, a serious person, say that AI was more dangerous than nuclear weapons, arguing for it to be regulated somehow.

CHAPTER 35

Reading Books

IN THE SUMMER of 1968 I had four weeks of programming classes, but the rest of my time I spent reading Science Fiction stories. I felt like I read all of Robert Heinlein's books, but of course that's impossible, he wrote so many. I borrowed from a nearby library the complete Robot Stories of Isaac Asimov. In it he lays out the Three Laws of Robotics. I think if it comes to the government regulating AI, they should probably start with that.

Speaking of Science Fiction, which I had been reading most of my life, beginning with Superman Comics, which I definitely think qualify as Science Fiction, there are often computers in stories about the future. I think I even read one or two books where there was a Programmer in the story. I didn't know what that was, but I thought it sounded cool. So, at 17, when I had my chance to become a Programmer, I was kind of primed for it. Programming computers, especially the old, big ones, and then with all the fantastic advances in technology that I witnessed on my various jobs, it was like Science Fiction coming true.

On the other hand, I really hate it when the villain in a movie is a Programmer, like the one in Jurassic Park. Programmers have a kind of bad reputation for being arrogant, but I've never seen one like that, with his millions of lines of code and his total lack of morality. That's not real. The little girl in the movie was a hero when she was trying to use the computer to either close the doors so the dinosaurs couldn't get in or open the doors so they could get out, I don't remember which, and she looked at the screen and said something like, "*I know this. It's*

UNIX." What was on the screen, though, was some graphical depiction of the file system that was also not real. It was an artist's concept because the way real file systems look to a Programmer is way too boring for normal people. And for people who are not Programmers, when you see a computer screen in a movie that is full of zeros and ones scrolling by, that's not real either. No one would ever do that. You can't read zeros and ones. I've often read memory and file dumps in binary, but always either in octal or hexadecimal. In case you don't know, those are other base two number systems.

About reading, I've mentioned reading computer manuals, books about programming, technical journals, etc., and I've also talked about how a Programmer is always learning, but so far I haven't put them together. Imagining someone wanting to be a Programmer, maybe studying Computer Science in school, or maybe already in a programming job, I've been trying to pass on lessons I've learned along the way that I believe could be helpful. Some of these lessons might seem far removed from programming if you see it as mainly coding. I've always said that coding is the easy part, a child could do it. The harder parts are design and problem solving. But there's even more to it than that. I think just about every job I've had involved learning something new to me. Either the computer was new, or the operating system, or the programming language, or the type of application, or the working environment, or maybe all of them. The first thing you do on a new programming job is learn new things, and the way you do a lot of that is by reading. Even after you're on the job things keep changing, so you never get to the point where you know everything and you can stop learning. That means you're always reading not only to get ahead, but even to just keep up. If you fall behind technically, you're likely going to be replaced.

When I was a young child, I read comic books continually, the ones for children, like Donald Duck, Richie Rich, Baby Huey, and many more. Some people have trouble learning to read, but I don't even remember it. It seems to me I could always read well, although I know I didn't learn to read until I went to school in the first grade. When I got a little older, I read Archie comics, then Superman and all the other super heroes, and then all the Marvel comics. I read MAD Magazine every month. Nobody told me to do that. In fact, it seems like a lot of people look down on comics as some kind of waste of time. Maybe because of the pictures, they don't take comics seriously. I liked the pictures, of course, but I read every word of the stories from beginning to end. Superman comics, as science fiction, used a lot of technical terms, some of them made up. I carefully read each one. Later, when I started reading books, I did the same thing, that is, I read every word from beginning to end, even long words that I didn't know or were made up. If comics are a waste of time, I could say pretty much the same thing about most books.

When I was about 11 or 12, living with my mother and brother and sister in a house in Palm Springs, I found out that my mother had a lot of books. The little house we had had a family room that was a converted garage, and in the back of the room was a very large storage room with a lot of shelves. I discovered that all of the shelves were full of books, and I started reading them. My mother never encouraged me or I don't think ever talked to me about books at all. But I spent a lot of time by myself looking through the books and reading them. There were all kinds of books. I learned to count to ten in Spanish. I memorized the Greek alphabet. I read several books about Yoga. One time I made my friend laugh when I put my foot behind my head. I read all the Oz books. Did you know that besides the Wizard of Oz, the same author wrote many more? I read all the Tarzan books by Edgar Rice Burroughs. He also wrote books about Mars. I read several James Bond books before the movies came out. I taught myself to read music and play the piano.

One day I read an article in Reader's Digest about a man who when he was a boy, maybe about the same age as I was then, about 14 maybe, wrote down a list of 100 things he wanted to do in his life, and then spent his life doing them. That was John Goddard, who became a famous explorer. He was the first to travel the entire length of the Nile River in a kayak. He followed that plan all his life, and did most of the things on his list. Some of the things were ordinary, like reading the Bible and learning to play the piano. Some were very adventurous, like climbing the highest mountains. One thing I remember he did not do was go to the Moon.

I was very impressed by that story, so John Goddard was a hero of mine. A hero is someone you wish you could be like, but you know you never can be. I never made my own list, but during my life I've gone many places and done many things that I imagined could be like that. I had a pilot's license and I flew private planes by myself all around southern California. I was a certified Scuba diver, and then got my advanced certification. I went Scuba diving in the Great Barrier Reef in Australia. I've been parachute jumping many times, especially from Hollister where the drop zone was right over my house, in free fall from 14,000 to 5,000 feet.

In Egypt on a tour with a group from the History Book Club, I rented a horse and rode all the way around the pyramids with some natives there. The Great Pyramid has signs on it that say you can't climb on it because it's too dangerous. So, I waited for night, and then went around to the back of it and climbed up with a little flashlight. The blocks the pyramids are made of look like steps, but they're too big, and I had to climb up them one at a time, ducking down and turning off my light whenever a car drove by. My problem was that the blocks were covered with sand, and to get up to the next block I had to put my hands in the sand in the dark to scramble up. The reason that was scary was that I had been seeing pictures of the small, poisonous horned vipers that like to hide in the sand there, and I was worried about finding one. From the top I could see the other pyramids, the Sphynx and the sound and light show going on down below. These things were not part of the tour. I did them all on my own.

When I received a brochure from the Natural History Museum of Los Angeles promoting a trip to Africa led by John Goddard, I instantly knew who he was some 30 years after reading that article about him, and I jumped at the chance. I got to meet my boyhood hero and travel with him all around Kenya and Tanzania. A few years later, he led another tour of Ecuador, to Quito and the Avenue of the Volcanoes, including a cruise of the Galapagos Islands, and I went with him again. He personally autographed a copy of his book, *Kayaks Down the Nile*, for me.

To me, all these things are connected. Reading history books and being a member of the History Book Club led me to a grand tour of Egypt, led by the archaeologist who wrote the book about Akhenaten, by the way. Reading an article in Reader's Digest and being a member of the Natural History Museum led me to an African safari with John Goddard. Reading is necessary for learning, and learning is necessary for computer programming. Reading is important.

John Goddard's Wildlife Safari to

AFRICA

through the game reserves and national parks of Kenya
with an optional extension to Tanzania
June 23-July 5, 1994

MICHAEL DI LORETO

John Goddard is one of the world's most famous explorers and adventurers. Travelers enjoy the adventure, fellowship, and personal attention not found on standard group tours. His fascinating enrichment lectures prepare the traveler for each day's activity, and he frequently leads impromptu excursions into the wilds for those willing to follow.

"To dare is to do, to fear is to fail." This philosophy has characterized John Goddard since he was 15, when he listed 127 challenging lifetime goals, such as exploring the world's great rivers, climbing the world's highest mountains, running a five minute mile, and playing *Claire De Lune* on the piano.

He has now accomplished 107 of these goals, and logged an impressive list of records in achieving them. He led the first expedition down the entire length of the Nile River, which the Los Angeles Times called "the most remarkable adventure of this generation." He later matched that by becoming the first man to explore the entire length of the world's second longest river, the Congo.

The subject of numerous magazine articles, including National Geographic, Life and Readers Digest, John Goddard has been the featured guest on many television shows including "This Is Your Life." He has published an account of his first big expedition, "Kayaks Down the Nile," and is now working on his autobiography.

Join John for the Great Migration—one of nature's greatest spectacles—as hundreds of thousands of wildebeest and zebra migrate across the Serengeti Plains during the months of June—September!

CHAPTER 36

Artificial Intelligence

I WAS INTERESTED IN everything about computers and software. One of those things was Artificial Intelligence. In the 1970s, I was a member of the ACM's SIGART, the Special Interest Group for Artificial Intelligence. I read their journal every month. In the 1980s and 1990s I attended several IJCAI conferences (International Joint Conference for Artificial Intelligence) and COLING conferences (International Conference on Computational Linguistics).

In the old days, Artificial Intelligence was about pattern matching, natural language processing, machine learning and game playing. Later there were neural networks. It was thought that if a computer could learn to play chess, it would also be able to learn other games, and beyond that, it would be able to develop strategies for real world situations. Remember the movie *War Games*? What happened instead was that IBM built a computer whose sole purpose was to play chess, and that computer was powerful enough to beat humans including the world's chess champion. The machine was called Deep Blue. That was a great accomplishment for computer technology, but chess stopped being part of Artificial Intelligence. That's because the program worked by "brute force". That is, it was fast enough and had enough memory that it could simply evaluate every possible move and pick the best one. Grandmaster chess players can look ahead a dozen or so moves, and they are considered to be super intelligent. But a powerful enough computer can look ahead practically to the end of the game with no intelligence at all.

There was a theory that if a computer could simulate every neuron and connection in a human brain, it would be just as smart as a human. It's not really possible because although conceivable, a computer that powerful would be as big as the Earth, or something like that.

At still another ACM meeting, the presenter said he thought computers were at the maximum theoretical limit in speed and memory capacity. He said that due to the speed of light signals in wires in computers could only go so fast. It sounds foolish now, of course, but who knew in the 1970s that Intel would acquire extraterrestrial technology and regularly blow away all earthly theoretical limits to computer performance. No? Well, you explain multi-Gigahertz Pentiums.

A major division in Artificial Intelligence was Natural Language Processing (NLP). The idea was for computers to understand written or spoken human languages, like English, and to generate or speak natural language text. I attended a SIGART meeting at SDC (System Development Corporation) in Santa Monica where they demonstrated a computer that could understand someone saying "Hello" to it. It took a long time to process the audio signal, but it finally printed "Hello". Apparently, it was the first time a computer could understand a spoken English sentence more or less in real time. That was the state of the art in the 1970s.

Natural Language Processing is such a big field on its own that there were international conferences just for that, but renamed to Computational Linguistics. I attended two COLING conferences, one at Stanford University and the other at a university in Budapest, Hungary. I was more interested in this part of Artificial Intelligence than any other.

CHAPTER 37

Foreign Languages

I N THE FALL of 1984, I decided I wanted to learn a foreign language. I was working at JPL in Pasadena, and Pasadena City College was nearby. I enrolled in a Chinese class because I thought that Chinese was the most foreign foreign language. They only had two semesters of Chinese at PCC, but I enjoyed learning the language so much that in 1985 I enrolled in both Japanese and French, and I kept going. I was a student there for 8 years, until January, 1992. Pasadena City College was unusual I think for a community college to offer 10 different foreign languages. In all, I took 26 semesters of all 10 foreign languages, including: Arabic, Chinese, French, German, Greek, Italian, Japanese, Latin, Russian and Spanish, plus 1 semester of American Sign Language. I encountered the Dean in the hallway one day, and he seemed to know who I was because he told me I was the only one who ever did that. I was on the Dean's Honor List 5 times, and was inducted into the Phi Kappa Phi Honor Society.

I've said how after learning so many programming languages I was able to learn new ones with no difficulty at all. When I had a job using a language I didn't know, I learned it so fast I was productive in the language right away. It was because I understood fundamentally what all programming languages had to do. When I read a book about a new language, I could see it from the point of view of the language designer. I could recognize features of the language that were similar to features in other languages I already knew, and when there was something different, I could immediately grasp its purpose and know how to use it.

Since all human languages are spoken by humans, and all humans more or less want to talk about the same things, I reasoned that all human languages would have a lot in common. I had the idea that if I could learn about 20 different foreign languages, and if they were different enough to be representative of the major language families, I would be able to understand all the other 4,000 languages in the world. The flaw in my plan was that it takes a long time to learn a foreign language, and I keep getting older. I think my concept was basically correct, though. When I learn another foreign language, I'm able to recognize features that are similar to other languages I've already learned, which makes learning faster. That could be grammatical structures, sounds, and often many words. When learning a new foreign language, I always look for what I call "free words". Most languages have words that are the same as English with slight differences in spelling and pronunciation, or if not English, then some other language I already know.

Before I travel to another country, I study the language for 2 or 3 months. At a conference in Budapest, I learned a little bit of Hungarian. On safari in Kenya and Tanzania, I told the tour guide in Swahili, "My hoe is lost again", a sentence from my lesson book. In Ghana on an Earthwatch archaeological project, I told the local workers in Twi, "Where's a good place to buy fish?" In northern India for a yoga retreat, I learned Hindi. In southern India for a wedding, I learned Kannada. In Arizona for another yoga retreat, I said to the real Navaho Shaman who was guiding us in Navaho, "You work at the hospital." It turned out he really did work at the hospital.

BEAUTYWAY: Anasazi Canyons, Yoga, Hiking and Navajo traditions with honored Elders

March 22-29, 2008

March 22- Arrive in Phoenix, journeying to Sedona
We meet and greet at the Phoenix Int'l airport at 12 noon, heading out on a 2-hour drive to Sedona. En route we stop over at Honanki and Palatki ruins. Following check-in to our hotel, we'll have our first yoga practice in the evening and share dinner. Overnight in Sedona.

March 23- Oak Creek area and Flagstaff.
After breakfast, we journey to Tuzigoot Nat'l Monument and Montezuma's well, both of which were inhabited by the Hohokam and Sinagua peoples from 700 years ago.
We'll reach Flagstaff around 1PM, have lunch and check in to our hotel. In the late afternoon we have Yoga practice at a local studio and free time to enjoy the galleries bearing fine local and native artwork and the charming historic downtown area of Flagstaff before catching dinner together.
Overnight in Flagstaff.

March 24- Flagstaff to Kayenta via Navajo lands.
Breakfast and drive to Wupati and Wowanki ruins, both Hopi sites--near Sunset Crater. Lunch en-route and check-in to hotel in Kayenta. Late afternoon at Navajo National Monument with Grandmother Mary Williams, who is a Navajo medicine woman.
Late supper in Kayenta and overnight.

March 25- Monument Valley.
Early AM Yoga class and breakfast at the hotel. Today we meet Emerson Gorman, a traditional Navajo elder and ceremonialist. We'll visit the stunning and geologically awesome Monument Valley, where we will take a guided tour deep into the valley for a few hours by jeep. Following lunch on site, there will be extra time for hiking and sitting among the marvelous rock formations, and an informal ceremony with Emerson.
Late afternoon Yoga class at hotel, dinner and overnight in Kayenta.

March 26- Chinle, Canyon de Chelly.
Next to Canyon de Chelly, Chinle is an hour and a half from Kayenta. We'll check in and then go for the day to this beautiful, anciently inhabited place with it's numerous cliff dwellings, which were inhabited by the Anasazi (Hi'sats'inom), Hopi, and later Navajo peoples. A jeep tour is required to take us back into Canyon del Muertos, but we'll hike out over the land trail upon our return.

March 27- Chinle.
Today a sweatlodge ceremony will be given by Emerson.
After an early Yoga class and breakfast we'll meet with him for this very special tradition of prayer and purification. Overnight in Chinle.

March 28- heading back to Phoenix. We'll stop at a couple of places of interest on the way back towards Phoenix. Check-in and Yoga class at hotel in the evening.

March 29- Retreat ends after breakfast and closing circle.

celebrating the ancient ways

community & culture

open up.......
to your true nature

Phoenixyoga.net P.O. Box 2716, Aptos, CA 95001 (831) 728.8064

MICHAEL DI LORETO

For a cruise on the Baltic Sea, I learned Danish, Swedish, Finnish, Estonian and Norwegian.

At home, with Rosetta Stone and Duolingo, I learned Tagalog, Portuguese, Polish and Dutch. For Buddhism classes I was attending, I learned a little bit of Tibetan. I've also read grammar books about Czech, Slovak, Ukrainian, Romanian, Sicilian, Turkish and some others. If you added it up, I actually did study more than 20 different foreign languages, and I really can learn new ones faster. The trouble is that if you don't practice regularly, you forget pretty fast too, or at least I do.

For most of those languages, I learned the grammar, the writing system and the sounds, but I didn't really get much beyond saying "Hello" and "Thank you." Learning a language is not the same thing as being able to speak the language. The things I just mentioned can be done alone, while speaking always involves another person. That's difficult for someone like me who is friendly, but not very sociable. I've said that I get along much better with computers than with people. There are whole years I don't remember at all because I was working alone in some computer room somewhere. Being a solitary Programmer is not for everyone.

I've said that an important quality in a Programmer is learning: being able to learn, wanting to learn, enjoying learning. It seems to me it's easier to do something you like, and easier to like something you do well. One time on the JTLS project at JPL, the manager asked me if I knew any good Simscript Programmers. I told him to just get a good Programmer. A good Programmer can learn the language. I always thought learning new things was one of my strengths.

Another thing about learning a foreign language is that it makes me want to travel to the country, and traveling to another country makes me want to learn the language. Motivation is very important for learning. Otherwise it can be very boring.

CHAPTER 38

General Linguistics

I ALSO BECAME VERY interested in General Linguistics. That's the field of study of languages in general, not any particular one. Computational Linguistics is about General Linguistics for computers, sort of. Anyway, my study of General Linguistics was to me a foundation for understanding Computational Linguistics. I have many books about Linguistics and Language in general. Many of them are just about English, but there are very often examples from other languages. To me, foreign languages are the down-to-earth practice of what Linguistics is all about in theory. Does that make sense? Studying foreign languages helps to understand Linguistics, and studying Linguistics helps to understand foreign languages, according to me.

In the Fall of 1992, I transferred to the California State University at Fullerton and enrolled in their Bachelor of Arts program for Linguistics. I began as a Senior and through the Fall 1994 semester I took 8 Senior and Graduate level Linguistics courses.

In the Fall of 1995, having moved to Northern California for my job at Silicon Graphics, I transferred to San Jose State University and enrolled in their BA program for Linguistics. I was there through the 1996 Fall semester, but my only Linguistics course was called Historical French Linguistics. I also had 3 other advanced French classes.

CHAPTER 39

Colleges and Universities

I DIDN'T GRADUATE FROM San Jose State, Cal State Fullerton or Pasadena City College. Besides the foreign languages and Linguistics courses I mentioned, I took some other courses at all three schools that were either required for a degree or that I was just interested in. For example, at PCC I had English and Math that I needed to transfer to Cal State Fullerton, but I also had one semester of beginning Piano and the Aviation Instrument Rating Ground School. I was a licensed private pilot working on getting my instrument rating at the time. I never got it, though, because I moved away before I finished my flight training. I was in the Caltech flying club.

At Cal State Fullerton, I also had American Government, Introduction to Human Communication and Symbolic Logic. Symbolic Logic fulfilled the Philosophy requirement, but it was also really interesting. It has symbols and rules for manipulating them which are similar to a programming language. I was immediately expert enough to correct the teacher one time.

At San Jose State, I also had Modern English and Topics in American History, both degree requirements. I didn't graduate from any of those three schools because I never had enough of the required courses. At Pasadena City College I wasn't even enrolled in a degree program. I didn't even think of it because I just wanted to learn foreign languages. And by then I was already in such a high level position in computer software that I didn't need a degree for anything.

In August of 2017, when I left Oracle, that was the end of my working career. I was already getting full Social Security, so I just retired. I never completely stopped my hobby of learning foreign languages, although it had been 10 years since my last class at San Jose State. I was using Rosetta Stone on my computer at home, and whenever I took a trip to another country I always studied the language for a couple of months before I went. But now that I wasn't working anymore, I decided to get back to taking foreign language classes.

I enrolled in the College of Southern Nevada (CSN) in a course in intermediate Russian. I had had 2 semesters of Russian at Pasadena City College years before, and then I had about 3 years of private lessons at a language school in Pasadena called Poly Languages Institute. Of course, by then I had forgotten just about everything, but it's funny how when you learn something for the second time it comes much faster. It's like things you forget are never completely gone.

In language classes it's usual to talk about things that are kind of personal as a way of practicing the new language. Common things for students to talk about in class are their major, when they're going to graduate, and so on. So it came out that I had about 12 years of college studying foreign languages and Linguistics but no degree. Towards the end of the second semester, the Russian teacher, I think believing that I was a good student, told me that with all my credits, I might be close to getting a bachelor's degree and suggested that I enroll in UNLV, the University of Nevada, Las Vegas.

So, in the Spring of 2018, I followed my teacher's advice and enrolled in UNLV. For a degree program I chose French because I thought I would start with the most credits that way. UNLV does not teach Russian and they don't have a degree program for Linguistics. It was much harder than I expected because I needed a lot of general education courses, like science, social science, fine arts, English, and Nevada state constitution, besides the 7 upper division French courses. I graduated in the Summer of 2019 with a total of 217 credits. You're supposed to only need 120 credits to graduate, but most of my foreign language and Linguistics courses didn't count. Due to my high grades, either A or A- in all 7 French classes, I was inducted into the Pi Delta Phi Société d'Honneur de Français (French Honor Society).

In the Fall of 2019, having accomplished my goal, I went back to CSN and took the two semesters of intermediate Russian again. I still wasn't trying to get a degree, I just loved Russian. But the teacher again, presumably impressed by my accomplishments, told me she thought I deserved an honorary degree in Russian. Well, that was nice, but you can't really do that. But again, that encouragement led me to enroll in an AA degree program in World Languages at CSN.

From the Fall of 2020 to the Spring of 2021 I took 2 semesters of Chinese, 2 semesters of Korean, and 2 semesters of Italian. I was on the Dean's Honors List for the Fall semester and the President's Honors List for the Spring semester. I was inducted into the Phi Theta Kappa Honor Society, and I graduated from CSN with High Honors. My degree GPA was 3.900.

In the Fall of 2021, I went back to UNLV and enrolled in a BA degree program for Romance Languages. That's mostly Italian, with a secondary language that's either French or Spanish and 2 semesters of Latin. From transfer credits, I already had enough credits in Latin, French and Spanish, and lower division Italian. I just needed 6 upper division Italian courses. I graduated in the Spring of 2024. In all, that made over 50 semesters of foreign languages.

In the Spring of 2022, I went back to CSN because I had so many credits that I thought I could get a second AA degree in World Languages. You don't have to redo any general education courses when you get a second degree, and the language requirement is only 14 credits or about 4 semesters. I had that many credits in 5 different languages, so I thought I could get another World Languages degree. I took one semester of German and I applied for graduation.

But my application for graduation was rejected because you're not allowed to have more than one degree in the same major. That was annoying. Other colleges, like Pasadena City College, for example, have separate AA degrees for each language. The World Languages degree at CSN doesn't mean all the languages in the world, it's just a catchall for any one language. They let me enroll in a degree program for World Languages, but then when I had enough credits to graduate, they refused. After fighting with them and losing, and not wanting to waste all my credits, I switched my major to Philosophy.

With all my transfer credits, I thought I only needed 2 semesters of Philosophy to graduate, so in the Summer of 2022 I took Philosophy 101 and 102. I miscalculated, though, and I still needed 2 more. So in the Fall of 2022, I took another Philosophy course at CSN, and in the Summer of 2023 I took a Philosophy course at UNLV and transferred it to CSN. I was still taking Italian classes at UNLV when, in the Summer of 2023, I was awarded an Associate of Arts degree in Philosophy with High Honors by CSN.

CHAPTER 40

End of the Story

WHAT THIS HAS to do with programming is a continuous desire to learn new things and an interest in finding out how things work. In the computer business, things are always changing, and a Programmer has to always learn new things. It's also necessary to want to know how things work.

I had never graduated from anything before, not even high school. I was enrolled all four years, but I only finished the first two. Now I guess this all means I have to give up my special status as being uneducated, although I still haven't been trained to think correctly.

Michael A. Di Loreto
VM Technology Lead
Embedded Software Operation

HEWLETT®
PACKARD

Hewlett-Packard Company
19447 Pruneridge Avenue, MS 47UM
Cupertino, California 95014

408/447-4875
Fax: 408/447-3350

www.chai.hp.com

E-mail: michael_diloreto@hp.com

Michael A. Di Loreto
Software Engineer/Scientist
Embedded Software Operation

HEWLETT®
PACKARD

Hewlett-Packard Company
19447 Pruneridge Avenue, MS 47UM
Cupertino, California 95014

408/447-4875
Fax: 408/447-3350

www.chai.hp.com

E-mail: michael_diloreto@hp.com

Michael A. Di Loreto
Systems Software Engineer

Hewlett-Packard Company
19447 Pruneridge Avenue
Bldg. 47L, MS 4020
Cupertino, CA 95014

408.447.3705 Tel
michael.diloreto@hp.com

Michael A. Di Loreto
Software Engineer/Scientist
Embedded Software Operation

Hewlett-Packard Company
1501 Page Mill Road, ms 1603
Palo Alto, CA 94304

650.857.4534 Tel
650.852.8061 Fax
michael_diloreto@hp.com

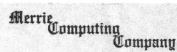

MICHAEL A. DI LORETO
VICE PRESIDENT

3452 E. FOOTHILL BLVD. • SUITE 340 • PASADENA, CA 91107
(818) 796-3044

HEWLETT®
PACKARD

Michael Di Loreto
Software Design Engineer
Internet Java Lab

Hewlett-Packard Company
19447 Pruneridge Avenue, MS 47UM
Cupertino, California 95014

408/447-4875
Fax 408/447-3350

E-Mail michael_diloreto@hp.com

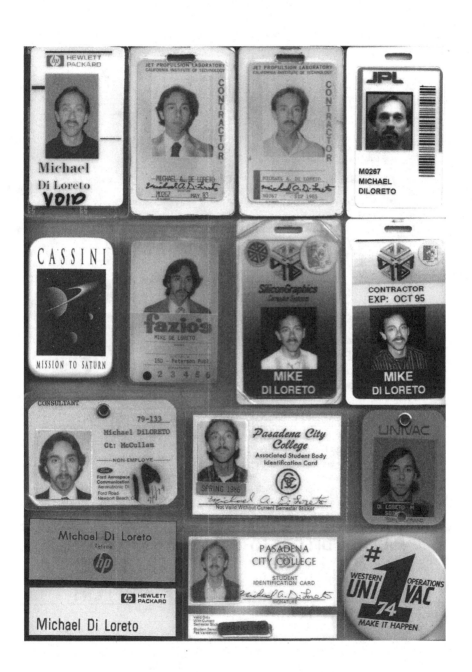

KEX
MICHAEL DI LORETO
SOFTWARE DESIGN ENGINEER
HEWLETT PACKARD
mdiloreto86   2028341

http://java.sun.com/javaone/

EX   02151999J60023
MICHAEL DI LORETO
SOFTWARE ENGINEER
HEWLETT-PACKARD

http://java.sun.com/javaone/

June 4-8, 2001
Moscone Center, San Francisco

MICHAEL
DI LORETO
SOFTWARE ENGINEER
HEWLETT-PACKARD
Badge ID: 02152001GC0228

EO

02152000JL0110
EX
MICHAEL DI LORETO
SOFTWARE ENGINEER
HEWLETT-PACKARD

June 6-9, 2000
Moscone Center, San Francisco

MICHAEL DI LORETO
SYSTEMS SOFTWARE ENGINEER
HEWLETT-PACKARD
1-134754

SUPER C++ TUTORIAL PASS

SD'99 • Moscone Convention Center
May 9-13, 1999

MICHAEL
DI LORETO
SOFTWARE DESIGN ENGINEER
HEWLETT-PACKARD

SD|99
software
DEVELOPMENT

SD CONFERENCE

Celebrating our
10th anniversary!

EMBEDDED 55772
SYSTEMS
CONFERENCE R

MICHAEL
MICHAEL DI LORETO

HEWLETT PACKARD
CUPERTINO, CA

EXHIBITOR

JavaOne Conference
HEWLETT PACKARD
Expanding Possibilities

chai

Michael
DiLoreto

EXHIBITOR

That's me playing chess with my Amiga computer at home. See how it has a color screen? The Macintosh at that time did not have a color monitor.

Michael Di Loreto
Programmer
Las Vegas
2024

Lessons

Here's a summary of the lessons for Programmers in this book. As you can see, they are not really technological. They are more like attitudes and behaviors that have all been proven useful in the author's programming career.

1. You can negotiate requirements.
2. Play programming makes you better.
3. Plan on things going wrong.
4. Let the manager try it.
5. Be more careful.
6. Get a smart tester.
7. Data visualization is valuable.
8. It's good to have a purpose.
9. Motivation is important.
10. Programming is a service.
11. Minimize the effort to correct mistakes.
12. Make your program human-readable.
13. Separate application from system code.
14. Build instrumentation in.
15. Don't guess.
16. Help others.
17. Learn new things.
18. Plan to write three more programs.
19. Don't schedule more than 50% of your time.
20. Let the computer do the work.
21. Read a lot.

Michael Di Loreto
Programmer
Las Vegas
2024

1. You can negotiate requirements.

Requirements are the beginning of any software development project. It's something like a list of things the software is supposed to do. They come from the customer who is paying the bills. The idea of this lesson is that the systems analyst should work with the customer to help them determine what can really be done in a reasonable amount of time.

2. Play programming makes you better.

A Programmer has assigned tasks and a schedule that's too short. There's a lot of pressure to get the scheduled tasks done. It's usually contrary to the manager's wishes that you spend time improving yourself. If you make yourself a better Programmer, you might get a better job than the one the manager wants you to do. Writing programs to learn things and to develop your skill might have to be done when nobody is looking, but your first obligation is to yourself after all.

3. Plan on things going wrong.

Murphey's law, if anything can go wrong it will. This is especially true for software. You should plan on it. Try to think about what might go wrong and what you can do to prevent it. You can't think of everything, but you can predict some things.

4. Let the manager try it.

If anything can go wrong it will, *during a demo*. Take advantage of this law of nature by creating an informal demo that if fails won't be a catastrophe. Doing this will make it more likely that a real demo will succeed.

5. Be more careful.

This is obvious for everybody, but software is so error-prone that you always have to check and double-check. Don't let there be any loose ends.

6. Get a smart tester.

Software always has bugs. Debugging is part of the programming process, but it can only go so far. If possible, get someone else to test your program, and get someone with enough intelligence to do a thorough job of it. Good luck.

7. Data visualization is valuable.

Programs have visible results that are the purpose of the program. But there are other aspects of programs that are not so visible, performance being an obvious one. Graphic displays of program performance and other related things like input and output data really help a lot for analysis and presentations.

8. It's good to have a purpose.

The work you're doing must have a meaningful goal in order for it to be personally satisfying. It also helps to focus on what you're trying to do so that you spend your time making progress toward the goal and not doing other things that take time away.

9. Motivation is important.

What motivates you more than getting paid? This may be more of a lesson for the managers than for the workers. Special incentives, however small, go a long way towards getting work done. Cash bonuses and awards really work.

10. Programming is a service.

There are a lot of Programmers who don't care about their customers. That's too bad. If you're doing your work for someone, and you care about helping that person or making them happy somehow, you're likely to do a much better job.

11. Minimize the effort to correct mistakes.

Mistakes are inevitable, especially in software. Know that you're going to make mistakes and take advantage of that fact by making ways to either avoid the mistakes or to be able to find and fix them without too much trouble. Remember, *"No matter how smart you think you are, the computer can always prove you're wrong."*

MICHAEL DI LORETO

12. Make your program human-readable.
There's some tendency in technical people to make their work more complicated almost as a way to demonstrate their superiority over other people. This is the wrong way to go. There is a way to make software that even non-technical people can understand. Ideally, your customer should be able to read your code.

13. Separate application from system code.
This is a special technique that may not seem intuitively obvious at all. In the book, there are a lot of examples of designing a language for programming an application. This last sentence will probably sound ridiculous to most people. How is that even possible? And if it could be done, what would it be good for? The answer is that structuring a program this way has many benefits to the quality of the software.

It's too much to explain here, but I sense an objection to the *design* part of the recommendation. That requires some creativity, and that makes it harder to do. Can that be right? Isn't program design an inherently creative activity?

14. Build instrumentation in.
This is another special technique for program design. It seems to be too common that a program is written and then debugged until it works. I call that negative debugging. That is, working backwards from failures to fix bugs in the code. That's very time-consuming. An alternative to that is to design in a mechanism for positively proving the program is right. A trivial example is having a gas gauge so that when the car stops running you don't have to work to find out why.

15. Don't guess.
Sherlock Holmes, the great problem-solver, told Dr. Watson, "I never guess." Well, that wasn't true, and he wasn't even real. Do you remember Cheech and Chong's bit about Sherlock Holmes? Hilarious! Instead of guessing, I use my own special two-step problem-solving methodology:

first gather all the relevant information; then solve the problem. Now you know my secret.

16. Help others.
Helping other people is obviously good for them, but it's really good for you too. You gain experience solving a wider variety of problems that way.

17. Learn new things.
A Programmer's job is to learn new things. That's what makes you valuable, and it's also what makes programming so interesting.

18. Plan to write three more programs.
Programmers are not good at estimating how long something is going to take. It's just not their natural talent. But managers want you to do it anyway, and they pressure you to make the estimates low. One way to think about how long a program is going to take is to plan on writing three more. That will give you a better idea of how much work there's really going to be.

19. Don't schedule more than 50% of your time.
Programmers are also not good at scheduling. This is similar to the previous one, but the calendar schedule is not the same as the estimated amount of work. If you're working alone it may be close, but there will still be things you can't control. If you're in an enterprise, a lot of time will be spent in meetings and doing other random things, like estimating and scheduling.

20. Let the computer do the work.
It turns out that there are always odd jobs you have to do that could be done by hand, but it's often possible to write a program to do them. Things like organizing data for analysis or for a presentation. This is a good opportunity to use different scripting languages. Remember, whatever you do is probably not going to be done just once.

MICHAEL DI LORETO

21. Read a lot.

Computer software development is vast and expanding. Your job as a Programmer is to be an expert at what you're doing. To do that, you have to keep up with all the changing technology. And reading is very important for that. But you think you don't have time. You're working overtime already. You're being pushed the other way. That's not correct. It's your responsibility to your company, to your customers and to yourself to be as good as you can be at your job.

Printed in the United States
by Baker & Taylor Publisher Services